MORE FIVE-STAR BASKETBALL BASKETBALL DRILLS

Compiled by

HOWARD GARFINKEL
and Will Klein

with Kevin Pigott and Matt Masiero

Contemporary Books

Chicago   New York   San Francisco   Lisbon   London   Madrid   Mexico City
Milan   New Delhi   San Juan   Seoul   Singapore   Sydney   Toronto

The *McGraw-Hill* Companies

Library of Congress Cataloging-in-Publication Data

More five-star basketball drills / compiled by Howard Garfinkel and Will Klein.
    p.   cm.
Includes index.
ISBN 0-07-141848-2
1. Basketball—Training. I. Garfinkel, Howard. II. Klein, Will.

GV885.35.M67 2004
796.323'2—dc21   2003053098

1 2 3 4 5 6 7 8 9 0 QPD/QPD 2 1 0 9 8 7 6 5 4 3

ISBN 0-07-141848-2

Interior design by Scott Rattray

McGraw-Hill books are available at special quantity discounts to use as premiums and sales promotions, or for use in corporate training programs. For more information, please write to the Director of Special Sales, Professional Publishing, McGraw-Hill, Two Penn Plaza, New York, NY 10121-2298. Or contact your local bookstore.

This book is printed on acid-free paper.

MORE FIVE-STAR BASKETBALL DRILLS

Also by Howard Garfinkel and Will Klein

Five-Star Basketball Drills
Five-Star Basketball

Contents

Preface

As head coach at the Five-Star Basketball camp in 1968, West Point's coach Bob Knight introduced the concept of "stations." Campers went through eight 10-minute skill sessions in each of the six mornings of their "Week to Live Basketball" in Honesdale, Pennsylvania. Since that time station teaching has developed into a Five-Star art form. They have evolved into four 20-minute teaching periods per day for six sessions, 12 sessions in all, in which campers go through each station twice. Combined with "Station 13," our optional individual instruction period each day, stations and lectures are the heart of the Five-Star teaching program as it brings the most dedicated, meticulous, and talented coaches to work with the most enthusiastic and determined campers.

Among those NCAA Division I and pro coaches who have taught and continue to teach at the Five-Star Camp are Hubie Brown, Rick Pitino, Bob Knight, Pete Gillen, Dick Vitale, Dave Odom, John Calipari, Herb Sendek, Seth Greenberg, Billy Donovan, Jerry Wainwright, Ed Schilling Jr., Mike Fratello, Tubby Smith, Jeff Van Gundy, Mike Dunleavy Sr., Richie Adubato, Tommy Amaker, Jack Ramsey, Larry Brown, Kevin O'Neill, Don Casey, Bob Hill, Mike Krzyzewski, James "Bruiser" Flint, Gene Keady, Dean Smith, Skip Prosser, Lute Olson, Roy Williams, Mike Jarvis, Gary Williams, Chuck Daly, and Jeff Ruland. Is it mere coincidence that NBA superstars such as Moses Malone, Michael Jordan, Jeff Ruland, Mark Aguirre, Reggie Williams, Tyrone "Mugsy" Bogues, Allan Houston, Jimmy Jackson, Alan Henderson, Alonzo Mourning, Patrick Ewing, Vince

Carter, Isiah Thomas, Stephon Marbury, Dominique Wilkins, Tom Gugliotta, Rasheed Wallace, Mark Jackson, Chris Mullin, Grant Hill, Christian Laettner, and Elton Brand have experienced these drills from which this book is culled when they were some of our illustrious campers? We think not!

In 1987, *Five-Star Basketball Drills* was published to help the aspiring player and coach in reaching his goal of being the best he could be. No matter what level he wanted to excel at—youth league, high school, college, or even pro—we provided a means for achievement. More than 100,000 copies of the first edition have sold throughout the world. However, our greatest endorsement of *Five-Star Basketball Drills* came from former Duke All-American and current pro Trajan Langdon. When his father was asked how Trajan could become such an advanced player in Alaska, not known as a hotbed of basketball prowess, Mr. Langdon replied that he had bought a copy of *Five-Star Basketball Drills* when Trajan was eleven years old and had worked with his son using our drills for about two hours a day for several years. Let it be noted that the game of basketball is currently growing by leaps and bounds in that state!

Basketball is an ever-evolving game. The three-point shot, isolation plays, and weight training, among other things, have revolutionized the sport. Consequently, the time has come for *More Five-Star Basketball Drills* to supplement every player and coach's hoop library. Our current staff of basketball teaching greats has described and diagrammed these new concepts and techniques for this book, which also includes drills from some of the most famous coaches in the history of the game.

MORE FIVE-STAR BASKETBALL DRILLS

1

Strength, Conditioning, and Agility

Dr. Jack Ramsey

Naismith Basketball Hall
of Fame

Speed and Quickness

Keys to Getting Runners to Run Faster

★ High knee kick, high heel kick
★ Nine-foot-long strides
★ Run with arms at sides
★ Head nailed to shoulders—doesn't move

Drill to Improve Speed (running workout every day—great warm-up)

★ Jog to half-court, lifting your knees to your chest on each stride. At half-court, continue at half-speed to the baseline using a normal jog. Keep your hands at your sides.

★ Jog to half-court, lifting your knees so you kick your butt on each stride. At half-court, continue at half-speed to the baseline using a normal jog. Keep your hands at your sides.

★ Jog to half-court, extending your legs by skipping. Swing your arms to help propel you. At half-court, continue at half-speed to the baseline using a normal jog.

★ Jog to half-court. Instead of running perpendicular to the 10-second line, move to your right at an angle of 45 degrees. On your third step, change direction and move to your left at an angle of 45 degrees. Change speeds as you change direction. (You are simulating V-cuts.) At half-court, continue at half-speed directly to the baseline on a straight line by using a normal jog.

Springfield Hall of Fame coach Jack Ramsey, winner of 234 games with St. Joseph's of Philadelphia and 826 games with the 76ers, Buffalo Braves, Trailblazers, and Pacers teaches Five-Star campers and coaches the proper technique to improve speed and quickness. His NBA champ "Walton Gang" of 1976–77 has been heralded by many as the greatest team ever.

Jumping

★ Move to half-court by jumping off both feet together, as far as possible on each jump; use your hands to propel yourself. Make sure you land using jump-stops. At half-court, jog to the baseline at half-speed.

★ Following the same procedure as above, work on quickness by jumping again as soon as you finish the previous jump.

★ Jump and touch the backboard with two hands.

★ Jump and touch the backboard with right and then left hand.

★ Using one foot at a time, continue to hop in place working on quickness. Vary the length of time you hop on each foot. You can perform this drill by hopping back and forth over a line such as the baseline or the foul line.

All of these jumping drills can be done with either a weighted belt or a weighted vest.

Agility

★ Figure-8 jumps in a circle

★ 2-foot jumps, series of four

★ Jump rope—300 jumps in two minutes

Physical Strength

★ Push-ups, four positions—25 times in each position: traditional, hands closed, hands pointed out, hands pointed in

Abs

★ Crunches—sides of feet together, hands on chest, lift head and shoulders off the floor
★ Side crunches—both sides

Legs

★ Leg extensions
★ Lunges (power walk)

Ed Schilling Jr.

Five-Star Basketball Camp

Explode to the Next Level

The following drills will allow you to reach your full potential as an athlete with regard to quickness, speed, and explosiveness, if they are done with high-level intensity and consistency over time.

Drill 1: Jump Rope Simulation

10 seconds of each of the following:

1. Two feet shoulder width
2. Right leg
3. Left leg
4. Jumping jacks
5. Feet wide
6. Split legs forward and back

Drill 2: Line Jumps

10 seconds of each of the following, full speed:

1. Two feet forward and back
2. Two feet sideways, right shoulder facing line
3. Two feet sideways, left shoulder facing line
4. One foot forward and back
5. Other foot sideways
6. One foot sideways
7. Other foot sideways
8. Split, forward and back
9. Left leg forward, cross over line

Drill 3: Eight Double Leg Tuck Jumps

Medicine ball, seated chest pass

Drill 4: Eight Glute (Butt) Kick Jumps

Seated overhead pass with medicine ball

Drill 5: Eight Lateral Jumps

1. Jump off two feet side to side; jump as high and as far as possible.
2. Medicine ball, overhead pass with sit-up

Drill 6: Six Single Leg Tuck Jumps

1. Hold left knee up at 90-degree angle while jumping in air off right leg. Bring right knee to chest. Repeat six times. Then do with right knee up while jumping off left leg.
2. Medicine ball, figure-8

Drill 7: Eight Split Jumps

1. Start with left leg forward and right leg back. Jump in air and bring knee to chest. Land with legs split—right leg forward, left leg back. Repeat.
2. Medicine ball, rhythm drill

Drill 8: Eight Jumps with Medicine Ball (ball above head)

Take medicine ball around ankles, knees, head, and repeat four times.

Drill 9: Medicine Ball Passing

1. Jump in air and throw chest pass on your way down (10 passes)
2. Hop scotch—wide, together, wide, repeat
3. Jump in air and throw overhead pass on your way down.
4. Hold left leg to butt, jump in "star formation" on right leg.
5. Throw ball as high as possible, 10 times, catch high.

6. Pass and bend (squat-like motion) and throw immediately.

Drill 10: Back to Back

With partner, hand ball four times right, four times left, four times fake right, come back, and hand left. Repeat the other way, working abdominals and obliques. Must be done with high intensity.

Drill 11: Transverse Downcourt

1. Repeat stand broad jumps
2. Lateral jumps, right shoulder pointing to end of court
3. Lateral jumps, left shoulder pointing to end of court
4. Double leg zigzag
5. Split jumps—left leg forward, right leg back, jump in air, bring knees to chest
6. Switch and land with right leg forward and left leg back, repeat down court
7. Repeat jumps, left leg
8. Repeat jumps, right leg
9. Power skips

Drill 12: Stride Length

Run over foam barriers with high knees and heel kicks. As stride length improves, move barriers back (strive for seven feet between barriers).

These 12 drill sequences help develop quickness, speed, and explosiveness. Do them in short (10 second) bursts at maximum speed and intensity. To avoid injury and receive the most benefit, do these drills three times a week. Muscles can only grow when they rest after exercise. Also, perform the drills on a soft surface (i.e., grass or wooden floor), and concentrate on proper form—never be out of control!

Potpourri of exercises and drills at Ed Schilling Jr.'s "Morning Mini-Lecture" at Robert Morris College (RMC) in 1992.

Matt Masiero

Five-Star Women's
Basketball Camp

Agility Series

Purpose: To improve footwork, quickness, and agility.

Organization: Each drill is done at full speed to maximize the benefits and simulate game conditions.

Line Series

Each drill is done in 15-second intervals up to one minute. For example, the first set is 15 seconds, the second set is 30 seconds, and so on.

1. Player finds a line on the court (baseline, sideline, or free-throw line) and begins to jump over the line left to right, jumping with both feet together, knees bent, and hands above the head.
2. Repeat Drill 1, but now jump forward-to-backward.
3. Repeat Drills 1 and 2, but incorporate them together to form a box (example: forward, left, backward, and right).
4. W-Form: Player uses the same form as in Drills 1 to 3, but now forms a W.

Minuteman/Lunge Series

1. Player finds a line on the court (baseline, sideline, or free-throw line) and gets into a defensive stance. With the leg that is on the line, the player pushes off using that leg and lunges forward with the opposite leg, pointing the toe in the direction of the lunge.
2. Repeat Drill 1, but increase to two, three, and four lunges consecutively.
3. Repeat Drill 1, but turn and face the opposite way using the opposite leg to push off on.

Ladder Drill

1. Player sprints full length of the court in 5 seconds.
2. 3 lengths in 15 seconds
3. 5 lengths in 40 seconds
4. 7 lengths in 40–45 seconds
5. 9 lengths in 55–60 seconds
6. 11 lengths in 65–70 seconds
7. 13 lengths in 80–90 seconds
8. 15 lengths in 95–105 seconds
9. Repeat drill going down (15, 13, 11, 9, 7, 5, 3, and 1). Use the same times.
10. Allow for equal time for sprint and then rest.

Pete McLean

Director of the Ultimate
Training Performance Center
South Salem, New York

Introduction to Speed Skills

Any coach or player in the NBA today will tell you that *speed wins*. From Alan Iverson to Latrell Sprewell, the players who are making the biggest impact on the modern game combine explosive speed, agility, and quickness to complete the scope of their game. To be a successful high school coach you need to incorporate a speed aspect into your game plan. Because the high school coach cannot recruit speed, this skill must be developed using cutting-edge training programs. Following are some of the important drills and concepts that will help you incorporate a speed, agility, and quickness program into your practice schedule. This clinic will address two of the most important topics "Speed Wins" stresses in our speed development program: *running mechanics* and *developing an explosive first step*.

Top speed is not the skill we want to teach in a basketball program. It is rare for a basketball player to reach top speed in the course of a game. But a player must be able to start, stop, and change direction with precision, explosion, and authority. There are two components that must be trained for athletes to incorporate these skills into their game: we have to stimulate both the musculoskeletal system and the neurological pathways that control the motor skills we are training. If a player has either muscular weakness or a neurological deficiency, full speed potential will never be realized. When "Speed Wins" trains athletes we concentrate on developing the proper motor skills first; then we work on the muscular component. This allows the body to adapt to the new skills in a nonfatigued state. Fatigue is the enemy of efficient motor skills. Once the athlete has learned the skills to perfection, we can incorporate a conditioning and power component to the training. Remember: perfect training leads to perfect performance.

Form Running

The first skill "Speed Wins" trains is proper running form. Most young athletes do not run correctly. They display poor upper body mechanics and posture and inefficient ground force development. The following simple drills will help correct these problems.

* ★ **Arm Action Drill:** This may be the most important drill in this sequence as arm action is usually nonexistent in the young athlete. "Speed Wins" spends a considerable amount of time on upper body form, but this drill will help demonstrate proper arm action.

   Player kneels on floor. Set arms at 90 degrees at the elbow. Hands should be lightly fisted and relaxed. Rear arm starts at the back pocket, front hand at the cheek or chin. On coach's cue, back hand drives forward, front hand drives back. This is one cycle. Repeat until perfect. The cue we use is pocket to cheek. We stress this on every drill!
* ★ **High Knees:** Knees to 90 degrees, foot dorsiflexed (flexed up), good arm action from shoulder, land on toes
* ★ **Butt Kickers:** Forward body lean, gluteus tight, heels to hips, land on toes
* ★ **Side Sliders:** Low hips (defensive position), feet parallel, and stay on toes
* ★ **Backward Shuffle:** Low hips, forward body lean, drive with proper arm action
* ★ **Carioca:** Keep hips square to front, try to achieve good counter action between upper and lower body, smooth precise feet, stay on toes.
* ★ **Fast Feet Drill:** Cue "quick feet." We stress soft foot plant, coordinated upper and lower body, feet no more than six inches off the ground.

Force Development

To ensure a more explosive first step, each stride cycle must be as efficient as possible. Every time the foot makes contact with the playing surface, maximum power must be attained. You may have the strongest athlete in the league, but if he or she can not transfer this strength to the foot strike point, all of this strength is wasted. Following are some of the drills we use to improve ground force mechanics and the explosive first step.

- ★ **Wheeling Drill:** This drill is done while leaning against a wall, arms fully extended, torso at about a 60-degree angle. Athlete brings one knee up to 90 degrees. On cue, drive the foot down to the ground, scrape the sole of the shoe against the ground, and then bring knee around to the start position. This is one cycle. We describe the action as "scraping dirt off of the sole of the shoe," and the action of the leg will be rotational. The drill should be done very deliberately and with explosive action, 10 to 20 cycles on each side.

- ★ **Power Stride:** The athlete lines up with feet parallel, hip-width apart, and arms at sides. On cue the athlete takes one explosive step out in perfect running position, head up, back leg extended, chest over front knee. The rear ankle, knee, hip, and shoulders must line up at between 45 to 50 degrees. Repeat this drill until it is perfect. Be sure to note the arm position. Check to ensure countered arms and legs, 90 degrees at elbow joint, and pocket to cheek (see above).

- ★ **Two-Step Power Stride:** This drill is the same as the power stride but continues with the other leg. Be sure to check that athlete does not overstride. The chest should be over the foot. If the foot is set beyond the chest, the stride is too long and will reinforce bad mechanics. Be sure to cue the arm action. Ten repeats on each side.

★ **Bounding:** From neutral position, drive the lead foot and leap. On contact alternate feet and bound 20 yards. This drill will trigger the neural systems to react quickly to stimulus from the ground. For the athlete to properly execute this drill, he or she must generate high forces and propel the foot to the ground forcefully. Coach should correct any athlete that double hops or skips. This drill must stress a single quick touch on each foot contact. When bounding is successfully attempted, the athlete will look as if he or she is power running. Do three to four sequences of 20 yards each.

★ **Power Stride-Bound:** Athlete will perform power stride and continue into a bound. This is a very difficult drill for the novice, so be prepared to spend some time working on the mechanics of this drill. The power stride-bound incorporates all of the concepts we have spoken about in the clinic. We stress proper mechanics; good arm action; driving from the toes; explosive, precise leg drive; and quick turnover. This will be the final drill in this drill sequence.

You should try to incorporate these drills into the beginning of the practice session so that all of the neural components are stimulated and ready for the remainder of the training session. These skills

Pete McLean's "Speed Wins" program is a fixture at Five-Star's backcourt camps in Honesdale and Pittsburgh. McLean, an assistant strength coach of the Jets in 1992 and assistant football and lacrosse coach at Ridgefield (Conn.) High School, is a nationally recognized speaker on speed development.

work best when the athlete is fresh and mentally alert. As the season develops, these drills can become part of the conditioning or the functional warm-up of any practice. I also recommend that some of these drills be used as part of your pregame warm-up. The same principles apply to the game environment as to the practice session; we want the muscles to be stimulated in the precise firing order to maximize performance.

Agility Station Workout

Kevin Sutton

Bishop McNamara
Forestville, Maryland

How can I improve without picking up a ball? This is one of the most often asked questions. Most players think that they must either shoot, dribble, or pass the ball in order to improve their game. Well, how many of you are willing to work on those skills that do not require a ball? The game of basketball is changing—agility and speed are a must!

The agility station workout is an acceptable workout that can be used individually or as a team workout. By spending 30 minutes a day (two days a week), you will see improvements in foot speed, jumping ability, balance, and coordination.

There are nine station formats. The number of participants will determine the number of people in each station. Each station lasts for two minutes (2 sets at 30 seconds with a 30 second rest in between). While one group is working, the second group is resting. As soon as the time is up, they switch. When the two-minute station is completed, the group rotates to the next station. The entire agility station workout should last between 30 and 45 minutes.

Station Diagram of Workout (Figure 1.1)

Station 1: Bleacher step-ups
Station 2: Foul line to foul line stride
Station 3: Ladder 1: Quickfeet/run
    through/strides
Station 4: Extended rope jump
Station 5: Defensive slides
Station 6: Speed rope
Station 7: Four-square jumps
Station 8: Ladders: drum major/high knee
Station 9: Width of lane defensive slides

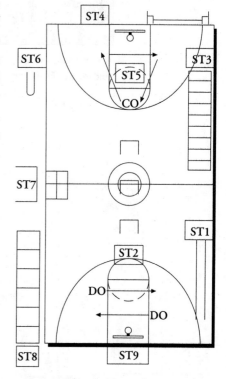

Figure 1.1

Agility station work performed by Honesdale backcourt campers in August 2002 under the guidance of Five-Star strength coach Talifarro Warren.

After every two-week period, reevaluate your progress. Then make changes in the station for three reasons:

★ To keep the workout exciting
★ To introduce new drills
★ To either increase the time per station to build stamina or decrease the time to develop more quickness

2

Defense

Keith Holubesko

Five-Star Basketball
Newport, Rhode Island

Complete Man-to-Man Defense Drill

Purpose: This drill is designed to put players in all of the defensive situations that occur in games.

Organization: The drill requires three people (passer at the top of the key, offense on the wing, and defense on same wing). The drill consists of defending all six situations, one after the other. Each player must execute the drill on both sides of the court.

1. X does not allow O to receive the ball when one passes away. If O catches the ball, X must stop the driving line (Figure 2.1).
2. X reacts to penetration by fake trapping (help and recover, Figure 2.2).

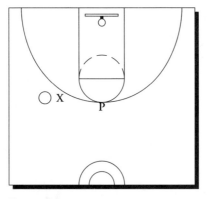

Figure 2.1

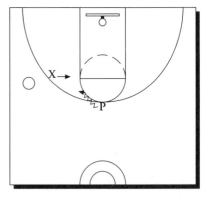

Figure 2.2

3. As P dribbles to the wing, offense goes to low post. X now works on post defense by defending the lob pass (Figure 2.3).
4. O goes through to opposite wing; X plays help-side defense (Figure 2.4).
5. P skip passes to O. X closes out and contests shot and driving line (Figure 2.5).
6. P looks to pass to O on a flash cut. X must deny the pass (Figure 2.6).

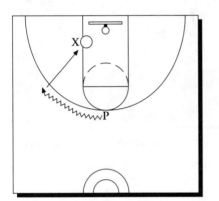

Figure 2.3

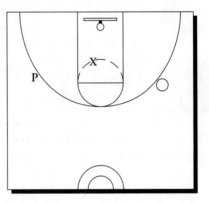

Figure 2.4

Figure 2.5

Figure 2.6

Jack Ramsey, "The Voice of NBA Basketball" for ESPN, demonstrates the correct footwork for the defensive stance.

Defense Drill Series

John Calipari

University of Memphis
Memphis, Tennessee

Purpose: To develop defensive footwork and change of direction.

Drill 1: Close-Out Drill (Figure 2.7)

1. Player 1 starts at baseline and sprints toward Coach 1 (C1) at free-throw line. Player gives a stutter step before reaching the coach.
2. Player 1 reaches Coach 1, breaks down into a defensive stance, and begins to lunge (stepping with lead foot) from strong elbow to weak-side baseline.
3. Player 1 reaches weak-side baseline and begins to sprint toward Coach 2 (C2), stutter stepping before reaching weak-side elbow.
4. Player 1 reaches Coach 2 at weak-side elbow, breaks down into a defensive stance, and begins to lunge toward strong-side baseline.

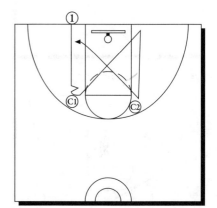

Figure 2.7

Drill 2: Lunges (Figure 2.8)

1. Player 1 begins in a defensive stance on one side of the free-throw lane.
2. Stepping with lead foot, Player 1 begins to lunge toward opposite sideline pushing off with the inner thigh of nonlead foot.
3. Player 1 repeats the drill coming back, so as to work on lunging with opposite lead foot.

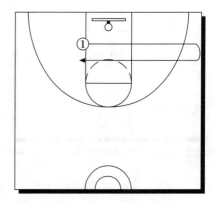

Figure 2.8

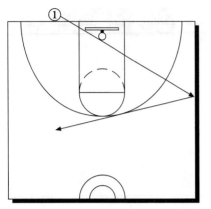

Figure 2.9

Figure 2.10

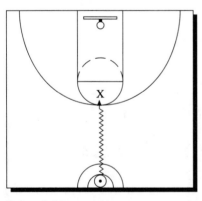

Figure 2.11

Drill 3: Running D/Change Direction (full-court—Figure 2.9)

Player 1 starts on baseline and runs on diagonal toward opposite elbow, free-throw line extended sideline, in order to to track down the offensive player. Player 1 then changes direction, planting on the foot closest to the sideline, and runs in opposite direction toward half-court.

Drill 4: One-on-One (Figure 2.10)

★ Using both ends of the floor, players go one-on-one from different spots on the perimeter (right wing, top of key, left wing).
★ Rotate from offense to defense, defense to end of line.
★ Change spots on the floor.
★ 12 players can do this drill simultaneously.

Drill 5: One-on-One Full Speed (Figure 2.11)

★ Offensive player starts at half-court and attacks the defense going full speed to the basket.
★ Rotate from offense to defense.
★ Attack from half-court right and left sides.

John Calipari prepares his defenders for "The Lunge" at Camp Bryn Mawr in Honesdale, Pennsylvania, in August 2002. An important drill and concept if you believe Coach Cal's theory that you can't stop the Iversons of this world with a simple slide step. Calipari took the University of Massachusetts from worst to first, rejuvenated the Nets in 1996, and guided Memphis to the NIT title in 2002, his second year at the helm.

Mike Fratello

NBA Analyst, TNT Network

Defensive Trap Drills

Purpose: To develop the correct defensive rotations when trapping in half-court.

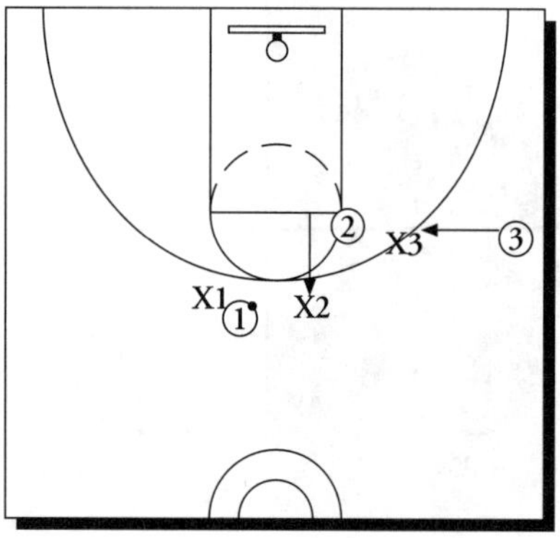

Figure 2.12

Drill 1: Trap Top (Figure 2.12)

1. Player 1 has the ball at step above top of key; Player 2 is at high strong-side elbow; Player 3 is at right wing.
2. X1 and X2 defensively split Player 1 for a trap.
3. X3 places himself between Players 2 and 3 and anticipates the pass to either player.
4. Player 1 attacks X2 and X3 with a dribble.
5. X1 and X2 trap Player 1 while X3 split-defends Players 2 and 3.

Drill 2: Trap Middle (Figure 2.13)

1. Player 1 has the ball at step above top of key; Player 2 is located in left low-post area. Player 3 is located in right low-post area.
2. X1 and X2 defensively split Player 1 for a trap.
3. X3 now steps up in the middle of the lane and places himself between Players 2 and 3, anticipating the pass to either player.
4. Player 1 attacks X1 and X2 with a dribble.
5. X1 and X2 trap Player 1 while X3 split-defends Players 2 and 3.

Figure 2.13

Post Double-Down Drills

Purpose: To develop the proper defensive rotations when double teaming in the post.

World-class clinician Mike Fratello points the way to tighter interior defense as part of his "double-bubble" Five-Star lectures in July 2001. The coach, who guided the Cavs and the Hawks to nine NBA play-off berths in 13 campaigns and recently completed his thirty-third Five-Star summer, was inducted into the camp's Hall of Fame on July 18, 2001.

Drill 1: Double Down
(top—Figure 2.14)

1. Coach (C) has ball on left wing; Player 5 is in low post on left side for offense.
2. X5 is matched up with Player 5; X4 is at free-throw line guarding Player 4.
3. Coach passes to Player 5 and X4 immediately doubles down from the top on the high side and protects the middle.

Figure 2.14

Figure 2.15

Drill 2: Double Down (top) and Rotate (Figure 2.15)

1. Same as Drill 1, except Player 3 is on the opposite (right) wing being guarded by X3.
2. As Coach passes to Player 5, X4 doubles down with X5.
3. X3 must now rotate to the middle of the lane and at least to the bottom of the free-throw circle so he can split Players 4 and 3.

Guard-to-Guard Screen and Pick-and-Roll Drill

Roberto Thompson

Five-Star Basketball

Purpose: This drill is designed to teach your players how to defend two scenarios of on-the-ball screens: guard-to-guard and post pick-and-roll.

Situation 1 (Figure 2.16)

1. Posts line up in the middle, guards on the sides.
2. Point guard (1) has ball on wing, offensive shooting guard is in the corner, offensive post is at the top of the key. All three players have defenders on them.
3. Player 1 dribbles to corner, where player 2 sets screen on ball.

Defense: You can teach to fight over the screen, with a hedge move from other defender, or you can switch guard-to-guard screen, with a go call from the defender that will pick up a man with the ball. Teach communication between defenders. Player X1 can go over or under the screen depending on the shooting ability of the point guard. Player X2 can hedge and recover or switch, and player X5 can also help and recover. If the offensive point guard goes away from the screen, there is no switch.

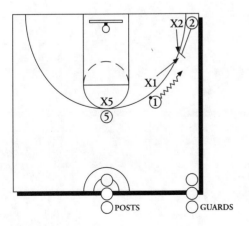

Figure 2.16

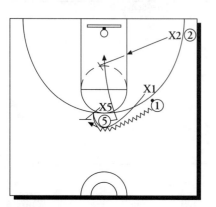

Figure 2.17

Situation 2: Trapping Pick-and-Roll (Figure 2.17)

1. Player X5 steps up and challenges the ball.
2. Player X1 comes over the top of the screen; because post is rolling, player X1 will get screened and will be unable to recover.
3. Player X1 then locks legs behind player X5 to trap the ball.
4. Player X2 comes from help position (one foot in the lane) to a position to front the offensive post, who is now rolling to the basket.

Defense: If pass goes to the corner, everyone recovers back to his man.

Twelve-Game Defensive Drill

Scott Bogumil

Gordon Tech High School
Chicago

Purpose: The purpose of this drill is to emphasize defensive deflections and offensive care of the ball (Figure 2.18).

Rules

★ Teams can score on both offense and defense.
★ Offensive team retains possession after a basket.
★ Loss of possession occurs on turnover or defensive rebound.
★ Two teams play five-on-five on half-court. Coaches referee and assign points.
★ First team to 12 points wins the game, play best two out of three games.

Points are awarded as follows:

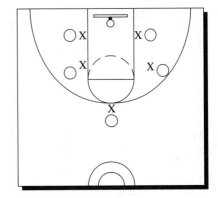

Figure 2.18

Offense—2 points for 2-point field goal, 3 points for 3-point field goal, 1 point for being fouled by defensive team.

Defense—1 point for deflection of pass, 1 point for defensive rebound, 1 point for a steal, 1 point for a turnover, 2 points for taking a charge.

Daryn Freedman

Brimmer and May School
Chestnut Hill, Massachusetts

The Ultimate Hustle Drill

Purpose: This drill emphasizes the importance of hustle in every game and can be done every day during practice. There are six parts to this drill (Figure 2.19).

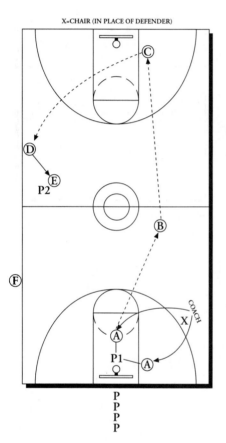

X=CHAIR (IN PLACE OF DEFENDER)

Figure 2.19

1. *Take the charge:* Player 1 will start in help position then step into position to take a charge from the coach (A). The charge can either be baseline or middle of the lane, depending on which way the coach goes. Proper technique should be emphasized:

   ★ Take first contact in the chest.
   ★ Fall backward so player lands on his butt and slides.
   ★ Once on butt, player should put hands palms down to help slide and protect his head.

2. *Loose ball dive:* As Player 1 is getting up from taking the charge, coach rolls the ball out to around half-court. Player 1 dives on the floor, grabbing the ball and rolling onto his back as he goes to the floor (B). While on his back, Player 1 passes ball to coach.

3. *Sprint for layup:* As Player 1 is getting up from the loose ball dive, coach throws a long pass to the other end of the court, so player must sprint in order to stop ball from going out of bounds and catch the ball in stride to make a layup (C).

4. *Save the ball:* After making a layup, Player 1 passes the ball to Player 2, who is around half-court. Player 2 bounces the ball so it is heading out of bounds and yells Player 1's name so Player 1 knows where Player 2 is. Player 1 then jumps from inbounds, grabs the ball, and makes the pass to Player 2

before either he or the ball goes out of bounds (D). While making the save, Player 1 calls Player 2's name, so Player 2 knows to go to the ball. After completing this part of the drill, Player 1 should take Player 2's spot when the next player in the line is going for the save.

5. *Catching the save:* After throwing the ball to save and yelling Player 1's name, Player 2 goes to the ball as Player 1 makes the save (E). This is done to prevent a defender from stealing the save. After catching the save, Player 2 passes the ball back to the coach.

6. *Push-ups and crunches:* After catching the save and passing the ball back to the coach, Player 2 proceeds to a designated area of the court where he does 20 push-ups and 20 crunches (F).

It is best to do this drill with two balls, so that after the coach passes the ball for the layup, he can get the other ball and start the next player.

Mitch Buonaguro

Five-Star Basketball Camp

Close-Out Drill Series

Purpose: To learn to close out on the perimeter, contest shot, and prevent dribble penetration.

Close-Out Drill with Contest

Part 1 (Figure 2.20)

1. Player 1 is offensive player on wing. Player 2 is defender with the ball.
2. Player 2 begins drill a half step above the box.
3. Player 2 throws pass to Player 1.

Part 2 (Figure 2.21)

1. Player 2 must run halfway to Player 1 and then slide under control to Player 1.
2. Player 1 will shot fake.
3. Player 2 must come out with both hands up and contest shot.
4. After shot fake, Player 1 brings ball down; Player 2 must bring hands down to guard against drive.

Part 3 (Figure 2.22)

You can do this drill from different spots on the floor. Player 2 can start in front of rim and throw ball to Player 1 at top of key.

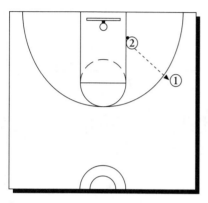

Figure 2.20

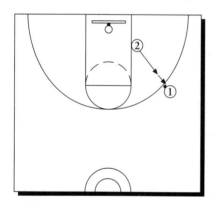

Figure 2.21

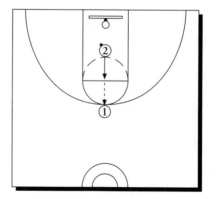

Figure 2.22

Part 4 (Figure 2.23)

1. The proper way to "close out" an offensive player is to run halfway and slide under control.
2. Come out with both hands up and contest shot.
3. Hands up to contest shot and hands down to guard drive.
4. Come out under control—don't get beat.

Close-Out Drill with Contest— Contain Drive

Part 1 (Figure 2.24)

1. Preparation: Player 1 is offensive player on wing and Player 2 is defender with ball.
2. Player 2 begins the drill a half step above the box.
3. Player 2 throws pass to Player 1.

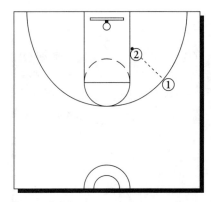

Figure 2.23

Part 2 (Figure 2.25)

1. Player 2 must run halfway to Player 1 and then slide under control to Player 1.
2. Player 1 will shot fake, and Player 2 must come out with both hands up to contest shot.
3. After shot fake, Player 1 will bring ball down and the defensive player will allow the offensive player to drive the ball with two dribbles in either direction.

Figure 2.24

Part 3 (Figure 2.26)

You can do this drill from different spots on the floor. Player 2 can start in front of the rim and throw back to Player 1 at top of key.

Figure 2.25

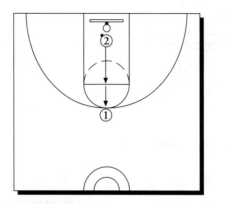

Figure 2.26

Figure 2.27

Figure 2.28

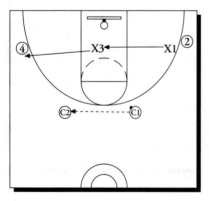

Figure 2.29

Part 4 (Figure 2.27)

1. The proper way to "close out is to run halfway and slide out under control.
2. Come out with both hands.
3. Hands down to guard drive.
4. Force ball to sideline—no middle.

Close-Out Deny with Help

Part 1 (Figure 2.28)

1. Preparation: Players X1 and X3 are defensive players. Players 2 and 4 are offensive players in corners.
2. Two coaches or managers are in guard slots.
3. Coach (C) 1 has ball to start drill.
4. Player X1 is denying Player 2 the ball; Player 3 is in the help position.

Part 2 (Figure 2.29)

1. C1 passes ball to C2.
2. Player X3 must close out to Player 4 and deny him the ball.
3. Player X1 must now run into lane and become help defender.

Rumeal Robinson (Rindge and Latin High School) receives private foul-shooting tips from Mitch Buonaguro at Pitt-I, 1985. Buonaguro, newly hired head coach at Fairfield, was fresh from assisting Rollie Massimino as Villanova upset Georgetown en route to the 1985 NCAA title. Four years later, Michigan's Robinson made two of the biggest free throws in NCAA tournament history in the waning seconds of overtime to seal Seton Hall's doom, 80–79. Buonaguro, a former camper himself at Brooklyn's Bishop Loughlin High School, would later rejoin "Daddy Mass" at Cleveland State. Mitch was inducted into the Five-Star Hall of Fame in the summer of 2003.

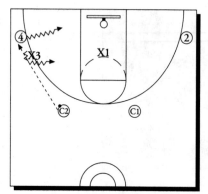

Figure 2.30

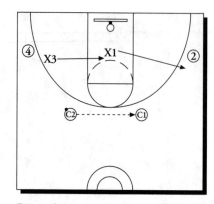

Figure 2.31

Part 3 (Figure 2.30)

1. If player X3 does not close out hard and deny, C2 can now make pass to player 4.
2. Player 4 can drive the ball and the drill becomes two-on-two.
3. Player X3 is trying to force player 4 to baseline; player X1 is giving help.

Part 4 (Figure 2.31)

You can continue drill by reversing ball: C2 reverses ball back to C1. Points of emphasis:

1. Defender working on closing out and denying
2. Other defender working on help side defense
3. Contain dribble, no middle

Defensive Stance Drill

Kevin Pigott

Fordham Preparatory School
Bronx, New York

Purpose: To work on defensive slides and transition from defense to offense.

Part 1 (Figure 2.32)

1. Line four players on side of "paint" facing downcourt.
2. Line eight more players on baseline.
3. Rotation consists of three groups, each consisting of four players.

Part 2 (Figure 2.33)

1. Each player in first group has right foot outside paint, left foot in paint.
2. On coach's command of "stance," players slap floor with palms, yell "ball," and slide to side.

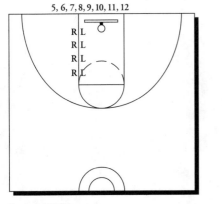

Figure 2.32

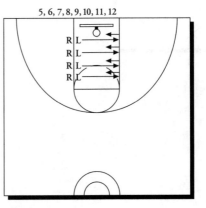

Figure 2.33

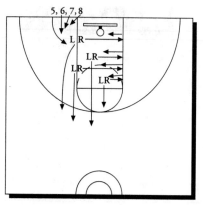

Figure 2.34

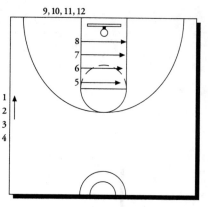

Figure 2.35

Part 3 (Figure 2.34)

1. On coach's command of "break," first group sprints to opposite baseline.
2. Second group replaces first group
3. Last player of second group yells "stance" when ready. All players get in stance, slap floor, and yell "ball."

Part 4 (Figure 2.35)

1. Second group slides until coach yells "break."
2. First group comes back on the sideline at half-speed.
3. Third group waits for turn in rotation.

3

Ballhandling and Dribbling

Rick Pitino

University of Louisville
Louisville, Kentucky

Game-Conditioning Dribbling Drills

Purpose: To increase ballhandling with dribble moves under gamelike conditions.

Organization: Start at half-court and begin to dribble full speed. Slow down (this puts the defense on its heels) and get lower at the foul line in order to execute the dribble move. After the move, explode by the imaginary defender body to body (known as putting your man in jail) to the baseline. You may want to use a chair to simulate a defender.

Dribble Moves

Practice these moves with both hands.

1. *Change of pace:* Dribble full speed, slow down and get lower at foul line, then pick up speed to go by the man body to body. Avoid going wide.
2. *Inside out:* Same change of pace principle. Push the ball to the opposite side and pull it back before it bounces. Keep your hand on top of the ball. Again, go by body to body.
3. *Hard stutter:* Again, full speed to foul line. Slow down, foot fire, then take off body to body past the imaginary defender.
4. *Hard stutter crossover:* This is a change of direction move. After hard stutter at the foul line, add a low crossover dribble to the opposite hand. Push ball past defender and go body to body.
5. *Behind the back:* Same change of direction principles. At the foul line, lead with right foot and wrap the ball around your back. Catch the ball with the left hand and push past the defense.

X performs the dribble moves twice (Figure 3.1): at the foul line and then at the foul line on the way back to half-court. Do three reps for each move with both hands for a total of 30.

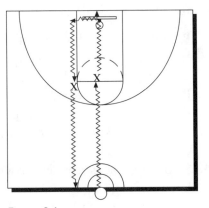

Figure 3.1

An attentive August Honesdale crowd watches Rick Pitino demonstrate his dribble move series. Six McDonald's All-Americans highlight the SRO throng.

Christian Laettner

Washington Wizards

Full-Court Layup

Purpose: To develop full-court ballhandling and cover maximum space with the dribble.

Minimal Dribble Drill (Figure 3.2)

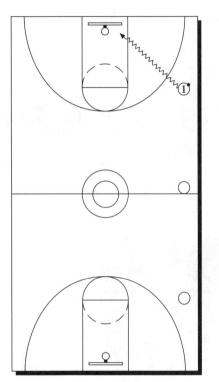

1. Player 1 starts with basketball as far away from the basket at top of key area on the opposite end of the floor.
2. Player 1 pushes the ball out and explodes to the basket in a three-dribble phase.
3. First dribble is from top of key to half-court.
4. Second dribble is from half-court to 3-point line.
5. Final, explosion dribble from 3-point line to basket for a layup.
6. Repeat going up the other side and switch sides of the floor.

Figure 3.2

After helping lead Duke to back-to-back national championships in 1991 and 1992, Christian Laettner of the Washington Wizards returned to his Five-Star roots, one of seven consecutive summers he either lectured or coached. Here Christian demonstrates his full-court dribbling artistry in July 1996 at Robert Morris. On July 30, 2000, Laettner became the second player to be inducted into the Five-Star Hall of Fame.

Al Rhodes

Logansport High School
Logansport, Indiana

One-on-One Basketball: Me Against You, Baby!

When you as a coach set up one-on-one drills, there are several things to consider:

★ The drills should fit your offensive scheme.
★ Your players should learn to go in straight lines to the basket.
★ Your players should practice the moves you want them to use.

Pick the areas on the floor you want to use. Restrict the area where the players are playing (see Figure 3.3). For example, just use the three-second lane. You can put tape on the floor to create out-of-bounds lines when the players are playing on the wing or from the corner. If you are a player reading this, you can use chalk on the outside court to create the out-of-bounds lines. Players need to learn to function in a limited area.

One-on-one should also be played off the dribble (Figure 3.4), from a catch of the ball, and with

Figure 3.3

Highly respected coach, motivator, and math teacher extraordinaire Al Rhodes uses geometric logic to explain his "one-on-one moves facing" drill at Station 13 at Five-Star in July 2001. Rhodes directed Warsaw High School to the Indiana State Championship in 1984 and racked up 14 sectional titles, seven regionals, and a quartet of semifinals in his 22-year career. "Country Al" retired after the 2001 season with 405 wins against only 133 defeats. He sent Rick Fox to the University of North Carolina and on to the Lakers among his 46 players to compete in the collegiate ranks. Rhodes runs the Five-Star Indiana Youth Camp (ages 10 to 15) in Ft. Wayne and was inducted in the Five-Star Hall of Fame in July 2003.

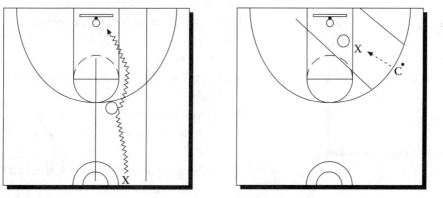

Figure 3.4   Figure 3.5

the player's back to the basket (Figure 3.5). It is important that you find out which players can play the different types of one-on-one. If you are a player reading this, you need to learn to play all of the different types of one-on-one.

Tony Digiovanni

Piscataway High School
Piscataway, New Jersey

The Half-Court "Chill" Drill

Purpose: This drill will enable you to work on an entire series of dribble moves at game speed.

Players start in the corner facing half-court with the ball in the outside hand (right hand according to the diagram in Figure 3.6). The player will perform a series of dribble moves at game speed and finish with a variety of moves. The player will perform the following moves at the particular spot on the floor.

1. Stutter step/change of speed
2. In and out
3. Spin dribble (ball should be in your left hand after spin)
4. Pull-back crossover—visualize a double team and take two crab dribbles backward to create space. Then make a front change (crossover) into your right hand.
5. Hardaway's Killer Crossover—between your legs (right to left) and then front change (left to right)
6. Around your back (ball should be in your left hand after going around your back)
7. Front change as you explode by the imaginary defender
8. Finishing moves:
   a. Layup off one leg, shoot it high off the glass
   b. Power layup off two legs, using your body to create space and protect the ball.
   c. Pull-up bank shot dropping the ball into the corner of the box
9. Moves for the more advanced player:
   a. Step back dribble move to create space—jump shot
   b. Spin-drop-step to the front of the rim and shoot a left-handed baby hook. On your hook, take the ball from your hip with two hands and put your left

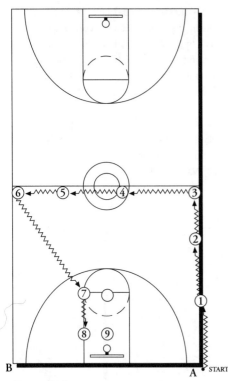

Figure 3.6

shoulder in your ear. Shoot it with your wrist and let the ball roll off of your fingertips.

c. Same move as b. above but fake the hook shot, pivot on your right foot, and step across with your left for a power layup (up-and-under move).

Perform the drill beginning from Corner B, and begin with the ball in your left hand. All above references to which hand the ball is in would then be reversed.

Piscataway High School's version of the "Chill" Drill ends with a baby hook demonstrated to perfection by Bob Hurley's assistant Tony DiGiovanni at Honesdale in June 2002.

Gary Manchel

Ohio University
Athens, Ohio

Individual Ballhandling Moves

Purpose: This drill will work on both conditioning and ballhandling. You will be able to work on a variety of moves at different speeds.

1. Start on right baseline (A) and do crossovers by each chair "C" (Figure 3.7). Start with right to left chairs.
2. At half-court, ball is in the right hand. Go hard at chair with "inside-out" move (B). You need to get to the rim in one dribble and shoot layups off two feet.
3. After getting your own rebound, attack the next chair with retreat dribble (C).
4. Now ball should be in the left hand. Past half-court, go left to right crossover to between legs at second chair (D), into jump shot off the dribble at foul line.

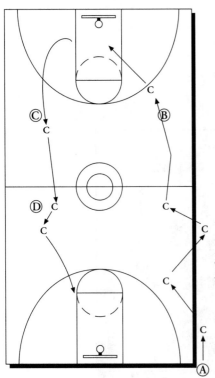

Figure 3.7

Individual Moves

Crossover

1. Plant outside foot slightly to outside foot of defense.
2. Cross ball over as though you are skipping a rock on the water. Hand should be on side of ball for crossover.
3. Catch ball quick with opposite hand to keep ball low and player quick.
4. Extend next step to go body to body by the defender.

Inside-Out

Now plant your opposite leg inside the defender's legs. Remember to sell the crossover by bringing ball to the middle of your body.

Retreat Dribble

1. Ball starts in right hand going hard to the chair.
2. Player imagines a double team and brings left leg in front so that it is "ball-body-defense."
3. Bring ball to back leg and quickly take defensive slides back (retreat).
4. Drop-step at 45-degree angle with front leg and cross ball over to the left hand.
5. Attack outside defender's legs going to the left.

Shot

Extend by the last chair with ball and legs and go 1-2 into jump shot. Do *not* lean or drift—go straight up-and-down on "J" or slightly toward rim.

Paul Hewitt

Georgia Tech University
Atlanta, Georgia

Georgia Tech Dribbling and Conditioning Workout

Purpose: To establish proficiency with both strong and weak hands in all the dribbling moves at game speed.

Drill 1: Game Conditioning and Dribbling Drill (Figure 3.8)

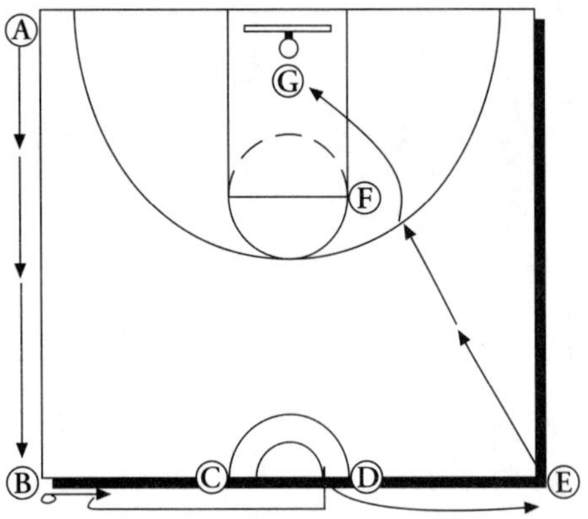

Figure 3.8

1. Inside-out (A)
2. Spin (switch hands) (B)
3. Pull back, pull back, crossover (C)
4. Half a spin (D)
5. Behind the back (E)
6. Any dribble move (F)
7. Finish (G)

Do this drill two times right and two times left.

Drill 2: (Do Drill 1 plus two others)

1. Go around—head, waist, knees, waist, head—five times, then do the opposite direction.
2. Zig-Zag—full court dribble moves—four times crossover, through legs, behind the back
3. 30 dribbles each (keep feet square and head up)
   a. Right: push and pull/back and forth
   b. Left: push and pull/back and forth
   c. Behind the back
4. Up 2 Back 2 (10 times)
   2 dribbles up, pull back, pull back, crossover
5. 20 dribbling moves inside the circle

Drill 3: Jump Rope

1. 1 minute—2 feet
2. 30 seconds, right foot
3. 30 seconds, left foot
4. 1 minute, alternating
5. 1 minute, 2 feet
6. 1 minute (anything you want)

Stan Jones

Florida State University
Tallahassee, Florida

Ups and Downs Ballhandling Drill

Purpose: Great drill for warm-up and conditioning. Works weak-hand finishing.

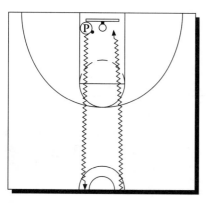

Figure 3.9

Drill 1: Ups and Downs—One Ball (Figure 3.9)

1. Player dribbles length of floor with strong hand then weak hand.
2. A cycle is one trip baseline-to-baseline.
3. Concentrate on looking at the rim.
4. This is a warm-up; therefore, the player can jog.
5. Shoot weak hand layups on each cycle (2 reverses, 2 strong side).

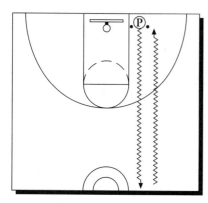

Figure 3.10

Drill 2: Ups and Downs—Two Balls (Figure 3.10)

1. Same as above except player has two balls.
2. Can add a zig-zag motion in this drill.
3. Can also add all dribbles as well (i.e., stutter, behind back, etc.).
4. Pick up pace to 75 percent on this drill.

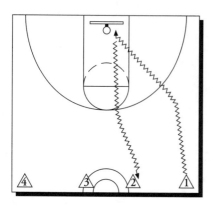

Figure 3.11

Drill 3: Dribble Moves with Layup Finish (Figure 3.11)

1. Attack basket at full speed at arc area, execute move, then one-dribble to finish.
2. Use all layup techniques (i.e., straight, inside hand, reverse, baby-hook, two-feet power layup).
3. Dribble out to next spot using same with same hand.
4. Perform same move at side of circle, other side of circle, opposite side of court.
5. Proceed to next move.

You don't have to be a guard to improve your two-ball dribbling dexterity, as shown at Station 5 in a session at Honesdale in August 2002.

Boston Celtics legend Nate "Tiny" Archibald demonstrates the "Up and Down" Drill to 2002 Honesdale backcourt campers. "Tiny" is the only player in history to lead the NBA in points and assists in the same season.

Passing and Screening

Mike LaPlante

Jacksonville State University
Jacksonville, Alabama

Low-Post Passing vs. Iso and Double Teams

Purpose: To teach and drill the lost art of feeding the post.

Emphasis and Teaching Points

* ★ Stress passing angles and passing away from defense.
* ★ Focus on positioning and post-up techniques in low post—"wide and low."
* ★ Emphasize catching ball and reading/reacting to defense—"catch with eyes and hands."
* ★ Passers learn to read/recognize how defense is playing post.
* ★ Perimeters learn to communicate off the ball (i.e., look and relocate).

Rules vs. Iso

* ★ Three-on-three on a side
* ★ Perimeter defense allows pass from point to wing/wing to point. Once passer has ball, apply intense ball pressure (Figure 4.1).
* ★ Low-post defense work on positioning to keep the ball out of post without giving up easy basket (coach's choice).
* ★ When ball is passed into post, low-post offense reads defense and plays.
* ★ Options:
    * ★ Attack with one-on-one moves.
    * ★ Pass to cutting perimeter player.
    * ★ Pass out and repeat.
* ★ On pass to post, perimeter player can:
    * ★ Offset/relocate
    * ★ Laker cut and fill
    * ★ X-screen and fill
    * ★ No help-side defense

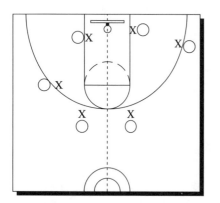

Figure 4.1

Zone—Circle Passing Drill

Purpose: To work on beating a zone defense with skip passes.

Points of Emphasis

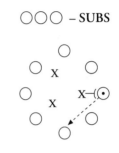

★ Passers anticipate next open man (Figure 4.2).
★ Move the ball quickly, when you can, to beat the defense.
★ Use pass fakes to move the defense.
★ Receivers show hands.

Rules

★ Passers can't pass to player next to them.
★ A tipped or deflected pass is a bad pass.

Figure 4.2

Former UNC-Wilmington star Gannon Baker keeps his game alive with player-coach duties in Iceland, Switzerland, and camps throughout the United States. His fierce passing station at Five-Star in Hampden-Sydney each summer cannot be captured by the camera.

★ A dropped or errant pass is a bad pass (fault always lies with the passer).

★ Coach always has a final say on good or bad pass.

★ On any bad pass, the player making the pass along with the two players to his or her right take the places of the defenders in the middle.

★ If there are enough players they can rotate from outside the circle to around the circle. The players in the circle on defense go outside the circle.

★ Coach may also use five-second rule.

★ Defense must pressure the ball to get five count.

Dribbling and Passing Series

Marv Kessler

Five-Star Basketball Camp

Purpose: To develop two-man game conditioning dribbling and passing skills.

Drill 1: Look In

★ Player 1 dribbles around the 3-point line looking into Player 2 in the post (Figure 4.3).

★ Player 1 changes hands as on the change of direction from right to left and left to right.

★ Player 2 should work on posting, sealing, and reposting based on the direction Player 1 is attacking.

Variation: add a player to middle as a target and when pass is made to the target, passer yells "shot."

Figure 4.3

Drill: 2: Drive, Pivot, and Pass

Purpose: To develop proper passing techniques after dribble attacking the lane and pivoting for protection.

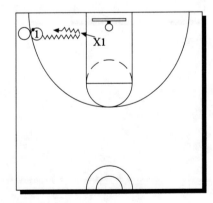

★ Player 1 attacks the lane with a left-handed baseline dribble (Figure 4.4).

★ X1 rotates over from right block to left block and stops Player 1 outside the lane.

★ Player 1 picks up his dribble and reverse pivots (on left foot) toward baseline.

★ Player 1 then passes to next player in line.

★ Focus on jump stop, pivot, and pass with outside hand.

Variation: pivot can be done on either foot.

Figure 4.4

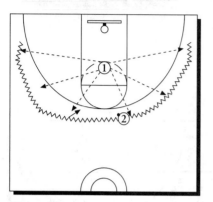

Figure 4.5

Drill: 3: Run Around

Purpose: To develop proper footwork and catching techniques after a passing is made.

- ★ Player 1 is located in the lane (Figure 4.5).

- ★ Player 1 holds the ball then fakes the pass.

- ★ Player 2 runs around the key and practices catching any pass by getting behind the ball.

- ★ Progress with the pass being made from Player 1 to Player 2.

Drill 4: Catching and Shooting on the Run

Purpose: To develop quick catching and shooting techniques after receiving the pass on the run.

- ★ Coach is the passer from top of the key area (Figure 4.6).
- ★ Player 1 must cut back and forth from left block to left wing, keeping his outside hand up ready to receive a pass.
- ★ Coach passes the ball to Player 1 at any time, yelling "shot" at his discretion.
- ★ Player 1 must properly catch and shoot.

Focus on catching and releasing the shot while on the move.

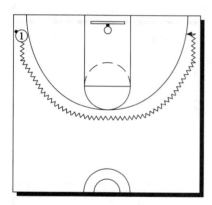

Figure 4.6

Post-Feed Passing and Relocation

Bob Hurley

St. Anthony's High School
Jersey City, New Jersey

Purpose: To develop passing to the post and moving without the ball (relocation) for a shot.

Drill 1: Pass and Relocate (Figure 4.7)

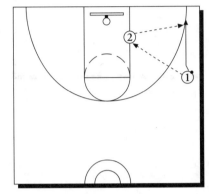

1. Player 1 passes to Player 2 in the post from the right wing.
2. Player 1 then runs to the right corner for a pass back from Player 2.
3. Player 1 catches and shoots.
4. Repeat five times.
5. Repeat left side.

Variation: catch and one hard dribble into a jump shot

Figure 4.7

Drill: 2: Pass and Relocate (2) (Figure 4.8)

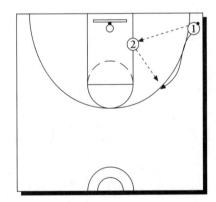

1. Player 1 passes to Player 2 in the post from the right corner.
2. Player 1 then runs to the right corner for a pass back from Player 2.
3. Player 1 catches and shoots.
4. Repeat five times.
5. Repeat on left side.

Variation: catch and one hard dribble, jump shot

Figure 4.8

Drill 3: Pass and Relocate (3) (Figure 4.9)

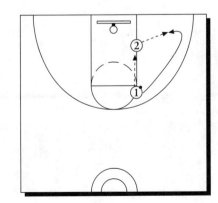

1. Player 1 passes to Player 2 in the post from the right elbow.
2. Player 1 then runs to the right corner for a pass back from Player 2.
3. Player 1 catches and shoots.
4. Repeat five times.
5. Repeat on left side.

Variation: catch and one hard dribble, jump shot

Figure 4.9

Figure 4.10

Drill 4: Pass and Relocate (4) (Figure 4.10)

1. Player 1 passes to Player 2 in the post from the right elbow.
2. Player 1 then runs to the right corner for a pass back from Player 2.
3. Player 1 catches and shoots.
4. Repeat five times.
5. Repeat from left to right elbow.

Variation: catch and one hard dribble, jump shot

Post-Feed Drill

Hubie Brown

Memphis Grizzlies

Purpose: To develop weak-hand passing to the post and proper catching techniques in the post.

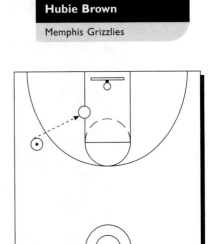

1. Passer feeds the post with weak hand (Figure 4.11).
2. Passer always feeds the post on baseline side.
3. Catcher always receives the ball with feet parallel.
4. Repeat and switch sides.

Variation: use bounce pass, chest pass, and wrap-around pass.

Figure 4.11

Few people lecture with the passion of Hubie Brown as shown in this Five-Star clinic in Pittsburgh in July 1988. The Five-Star Walls of Fame are in the background.

Hubie Brown's no-look, weak-hand pass during a July 2000 lecture at RMU augments this drill to perfection.

Twelve-Second Passing Drill

Keith Holubesko

Newport, Rhode Island
Five-Star Basketball

Purpose: Feeding the post is one of the most frequent plays in basketball, but many players do not practice it enough and end up creating a turnover or giving up on the play. The 12-second drill encourages patience and develops the skills needed to *pass into the low post* successfully.

Figure 4.12

Organization: Once a player receives the ball, he has a total of 12 seconds until he has to give it up (Figure 4.12). He has four seconds on the catch, four seconds of dribbling, and four more when he picks up the ball. This drill uses 4, 4, and 4 seconds to avoid closely guarded violations.

1. The drill starts with a player spinning out a pass to himself on the wing with a defender playing him (or imagine a player defending). In the low post is an offensive player (or imagine one).
2. After the catch, the player must sweep the ball low and step (pivot) to create space while looking to pass the ball into the post player.
3. Once four seconds have elapsed, he must begin to dribble. The player must execute an up two, back two, pullback crossover dribble for four seconds while looking to pass inside.
4. After four seconds, he must pick the ball up. He has four more seconds to sweep and step with ball fakes and pass the ball inside. The type of passes can be a wrap-around, bounce, an over-the-head, or a lob. Be sure to fake a pass to make a pass.
5. After feeding the post, relocate to get the ball back (fade, bump, or Laker cut).

Snap the wrist and follow through, as Fordham's Bob Hill orders for the chest pass.

This is a great drill that teaches a player to use his time efficiently, as well as to work on passing in game situations. The results are fewer forced turnovers and more successful low-post entries.

Freedom from the Press Drills

Danny Walck

Warwick High School
Lititz, Pennsylvania

The following drills offer three ways of attacking the double team (trap).

Key Points

★ *Passer*: Make sure you clear yourself from the backboard and baseline. Give yourself room to work.
★ Determine your location for inbounds pass to be received.
★ *Receiver*: Catch with your back to baseline and sideline. This gives the receiver good court vision. Teach proper footwork on the catch.
★ *Receiver*: Read the double team. What type of double team (trap) is it?
  ★ High and tight (defenders are together with trap toward baseline)
  ★ Loose (one defender is toward sideline and the other is coming from baseline)
  ★ Wide and tight (defenders are tight together with trap being toward the sideline)

Drill 1: Step-Through (Figures 4.13 and 4.14)

1. Catch with your back to the baseline and sideline. Find your offensive basket ("see the rim")—it gives you court vision.
2. Read the trap.
3. Ball fake bringing the ball to your shoulder on a step back move (the defense raises up).
4. Step through low, long, and hard.
5. Get first dribble down outside the double team.

Figure 4.13

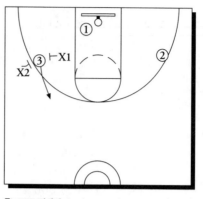

Figure 4.14

Drill 2: Wrap-Around Pass (high and tight or wide and tight— Figures 4.15 and 4.16)

1. Catch with your back to the baseline and sideline. "See Rim" gives you court vision.
2. Read the trap.
3. Attack one player in the trap.
4. "Fake a pass to make a pass."
5. Pass to inbounder (if wide and tight) using wrap-around pass.
6. Or pass to sideline option (if high and tight).

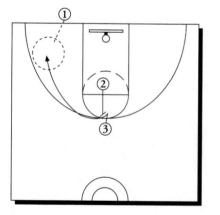

Figure 4.15

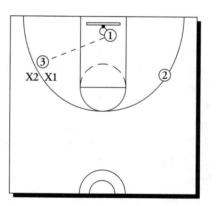

Figure 4.16

Drill 3: Spin Dribble Out
(high and tight or wide and tight—
Figures 4.17 and 4.18)

1. Catch with your back to the baseline and sideline. "See Rim" gives you court vision.
2. Read the trap.
3. Attack one player in the trap.
4. Step into the middle of the individual defender's stance.
5. Spin dribble out of the trap, sealing defender by getting your body past his knee.
6. Place dribble out in front avoiding the reach from behind.

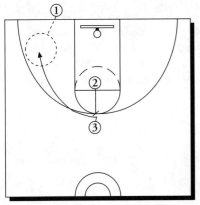

Figure 4.17

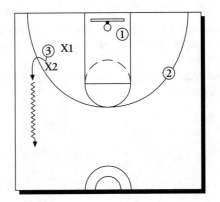

Figure 4.18

Getting the ball inbounds against pressure is one of the most underrated skills in the game, especially for guards. The always intense, always precise Danny Walck (Warwich High School) points out the exact spot on the floor for the entry pass in his "Freedom from the Press" drill at backcourt camp at RMU. Big guys should also pay attention to these maneuvers.

Rules for Screening and Using the Screen

Dave Odom

University of South Carolina
Columbia, South Carolina

Purpose: The objective of the screen is to get defense to switch—to create a mismatch.

Rules for screener

★ Set good screen
  ★ Knees bent
  ★ Shoulder width on feet, balanced and strong
  ★ Inside elbow (arm closest to basket) up
  ★ Other arm down, protecting ball
  ★ Perpendicular to path of defense (roadblock example)
★ 180 degree turn toward ball
  ★ When to turn? One step past screener
  ★ Be in position to see it and receive it
  ★ Slide down lane with target hand
★ Go to near box
  ★ Junction, intersection
  ★ Passer knows you're going there
★ Post man low after mismatch
  ★ Get layups—don't settle for jump shots

Rules for offense with ball

1. Set man up
  ★ Parallels setting good screen
  ★ Fake left to use screen right
  ★ Get defender low line of screen
2. Brush shoulders with screener
  ★ Moment of decision
  ★ Great guards see defense. Where is the third defender?
  ★ Stop and widen
  ★ Three-point shot or dribble drive banker
  ★ Read both defenders
  ★ Your man and screener's man
  ★ Know when to pass, dribble, or shoot

Dave Odom's screening stuff is as good as it gets, as shown here at RMU in July 2002. The architect of "The Miracle at Winston-Salem," Odom led Wake Forest to a pair of ACC titles in 1995 and 1996. Odom, who is rebuilding the South Carolina Gamecocks in his own image, was inducted into the Five-Star Hall of Fame in July 2002.

3. Take ball to corner to give mismatch time enough to develop and space enough
   ★ Pick 'n' pop instead of rolling
   ★ Separate and expand the defense to create space and mismatches

5

Individual Moves

Michael Jordan

Jordan Jab-Step Shooting Series

Purpose: To develop and utilize footwork for attacking the basket in order to create space between you and your defender to set up your jump shot.

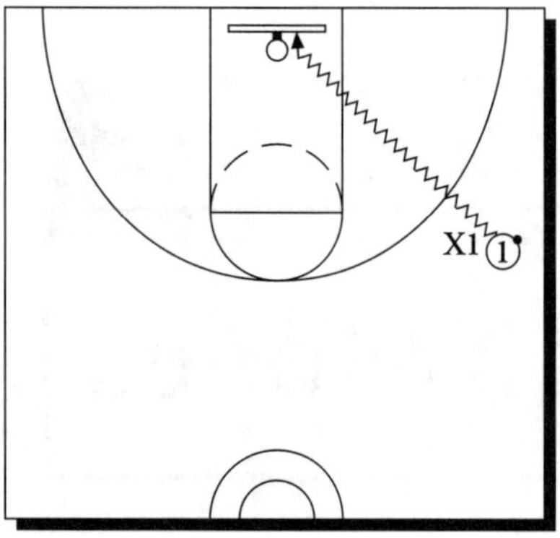

Figure 5.1

Drill 1: Jab-Step Drive (Figure 5.1)

1. Player 1 starts on the right wing against X1.
2. Player 1 attacks X1 up foot with a hard right foot jab-step.
3. Player 1 then explodes with a hard drive to the basket for a layup.
4. Done on both sides of the floor with both feet.

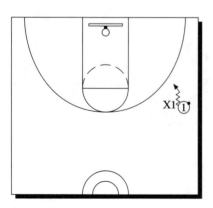

Figure 5.2

Drill 2: Jab-Step Pull Back (Figure 5.2)

1. Player 1 starts on the right wing against X1.
2. Player 1 attacks X1 up foot with a hard right foot jab-step.
3. Player 1 then pulls back hard for a jump shot.
4. Done on both sides of the floor with both feet.

Drill 3: Jab-Step/One Dribble Pull-Up (Figure 5.3)

1. Player 1 starts on the right wing against X1.
2. Player 1 attacks X1 up foot with a hard right foot jab-step.
3. Player 1 then explodes and takes one hard dribble right for a pull-up jump shot.
4. Done on both sides of the floor with both feet.

Figure 5.3

Variation: the one dribble can be done either to the left or right.

Low Block Shooting Series

Purpose: To develop low post turnaround jump shooting.

Block to Block Turnaround
(Figures 5.4 and 5.5)

- ★ Go from block to block shooting turn-around jump shots.
- ★ Mix this drill up shooting turnaround jump shots by turning toward both the right and left shoulders.
- ★ Start on both sides of the floor.
- ★ Square shoulders when shooting. Do not turn and throw!

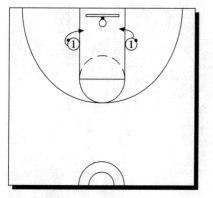

Figure 5.4

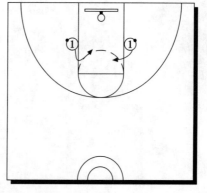

Figure 5.5

Rob Grinter of Louisville, Ky., is the greatest hoop technician that no one has ever heard of. Here he uses his tennis ball bit to emphasize heads-up dribbling and eyes off the ball, a unique lead-in to anyone's "one-on-one moves facing" series.

The Five-Star Hall of Fame was born on July 28, 2000, with the induction of the world's greatest athlete—alive, dead, or yet unborn—Michael Jordan. From left to right: codirector Howard Garfinkel, Michael Jordan, codirector Will Klein, and associate director Leigh Klein.

Two great minds think alike. Michael Jordan picked on the kid in the Duke shorts for his one-on-one demonstration during his lecture at RMC in July 2000. Grant Hill played defense against the kid with the Carolina shorts during bonus coverage at Station 13 following his lecture in July 1998.

MJ received a tumultuous reception from the more than 500 campers, 80 staff members, and hundreds of invited guests, media, and college coaches in attendance.

Ten to Get Open

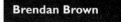

Brendan Brown

Assistant Coach
Memphis Grizzlies

Purpose: To develop shooting skills while using a screen and dribble moves. All drills should be done on both sides of the floor!

Drill 1: Use of the Screen (Figure 5.6)

1. Screener (S) starts underneath the basket on the baseline.
2. Take two steps up the middle of the lane (simulate setting up the defender with a fake cut).
3. Come off screener, going shoulder to shoulder in the mid-post area.
4. Receive pass from P and pull up for jump shot near left elbow area.

Figure 5.6

Drill 2: Use of the Screen (2) (Figure 5.7)

1. S begins with the same movements as in Drill 1, but after coming off the screen uses a shot fake.
2. Receive pass from P and take two hard dribbles to the middle of the lane.
3. Pull up for jump shot at free-throw line area.

Figure 5.7

Drill 3: "Iverson Move" (Figure 5.8)

1. S performs same movements as Drill 1 into the "Iverson Move."
2. Catch pass from P and utilize a reverse spin dribble with hand closest to sideline.
3. Continue with two hard dribbles to the baseline.
4. Pull up for a jump shot on the left baseline.

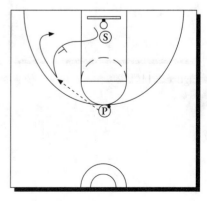

Figure 5.8

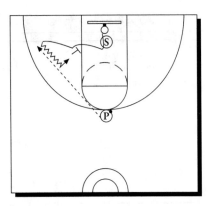

Figure 5.9

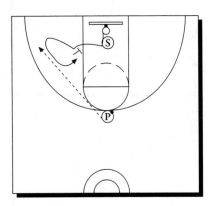

Figure 5.10

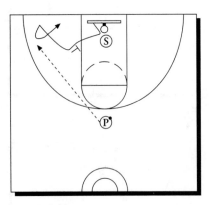

Figure 5.11

Drill 4: "Reggie Miller Move" (Figure 5.9)

1. S performs same movements as Drill 1, but uses the fade toward corner.
2. Cut into the screener nose to nose, staying low and pushing off your screener's waist.
3. S catches the pass from P on the baseline side, facing basket.
4. Use a crossover dribble and go back toward the middle for a pull-up jump shot.

Drill 5: "Reggie Miller Move" (2) (Figure 5.10)

1. S performs same movements as "Miller Move."
2. After pass from P, S uses two dribbles back to the middle.
3. S pulls up for a 12-foot shot off the backboard.

Drill 6: "Reggie Miller Fade-Away Move" (Figure 5.11)

1. S performs same movements as "Miller Move."
2. After the pass from P, S takes one dribble to the middle and then a second crossover dribble toward the baseline.
3. S pulls up for a fade-away jump shot on the baseline.

Drill 7: "Reggie Miller Fade-Away Move" (2) (Figure 5.12)

1. S performs same movements as "Miller Fade-Away Move."
2. After pass from P, S drives toward the middle with one hard dribble.
3. Take one hard crossover dribble toward the baseline.
4. S pulls up for a fade-away jump shot high off the glass.

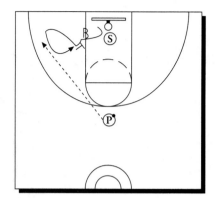

Figure 5.12

Variation: practice with a shot blocker.

Drill 8: "Reggie Miller Over-the-Top Move" (Figure 5.13)

1. S starts underneath the basket on the baseline.
2. Take two steps as to fake a cut up toward elbow.
3. Come off screener, over the topside, rubbing the inside shoulder against the screener's inside shoulder.
4. Turn your body toward P by using a reverse pivot on the inside foot.
5. Catch pass from P facing the basket in baseline area.
6. Pull up for a jump shot.

Figure 5.13

Drill 9: "Reggie Miller Double-Curl Move" (Figure 5.14)

1. S performs a two-step set move.
2. S then curls off the screener, shoulder to shoulder.
3. S continues the curl all the way around the screener (simulating a loop) and fades toward the baseline.
4. S catches pass from P and pulls up for a baseline jump shot.

Figure 5.14

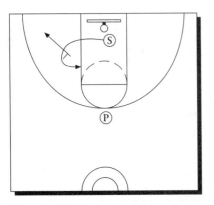

Figure 5.15

Drill 10: Screener-Corner Fade (Figure 5.15)

1. S performs a two-step set move.
2. S then curls off the screener, shoulder to shoulder.
3. Instead of S catching the pass from P, the screener now fades to the corner baseline.
4. P passes to screener for a baseline jump shot.

The apple doesn't fall far from the tree. Brendan Brown, assistant coach of the Memphis Grizzlies and son of teaching guru Hubie Brown and one of the brightest young minds in the game in his own right, turns screening, fading, and movement without the ball into an art form.

6

Post Play

Rick Pitino

University of Louisville
Louisville, Kentucky

Offensive Moves in the Low Post

Purpose: The following moves are used when an offensive player has his back to the basket while in the low-post area. A good offensive low-post player must have a variety of moves in order to ensure high percentage scoring opportunities.

The Moses Malone Move (Drop-Step)

1. Receive ball while straddling the first marker (not the low block).
2. Be a widebody with elbows out and ball underneath the chin. Execute a drop-step to the basket baseline side if being played on the high side. Drop-step middle if being played on low side.
3. While drop-stepping to the basket, take one low power dribble and be sure to point your inside shoulder to the basket.
4. Avoid exposing the ball to the defense.

The Kevin McHale Move (Jump-Hook)

1. Receive ball on first marker and locate the defense.
2. Execute a drop-step with a power dribble in either direction.
3. Shoot a jump-hook.
4. Be sure not to move your inside pivot foot.
5. The inside shoulder and elbow must be pointing at the defender.

The Bernard King Move (Turnaround Jump Shot)

1. Receive ball on first marker and locate defense.

2. Pivot away and execute a turnaround jump shot.
3. Keep ball shoulder high while pivoting and release when square to the basket.

The Dominique Wilkens Move (Up-and-Under)

1. Receive ball on the first marker and locate defense.
2. Plan to take a turnaround jump shot in the middle of the paint.
3. If the defender beats you, execute a shot fake and crossover step under the defender toward the baseline.
4. Take one power dribble going to the basket and jump off two feet for a layup.

The Jack Sikma Move (Reverse Pivot)

1. Receive ball on first marker and locate the defense.
2. If defense plays behind, then execute a reverse pivot away from the defender and take a jump shot.
3. The second option is to reverse pivot, fake the jump shot, then crossover step for a layup.

Drill: Individual Low-Post Workout (Figure 6.1)

1. Start by spinning out a pass from the baseline and catch the ball at the first marker.
2. Execute one of the offensive moves mentioned earlier.
3. Alternate sides.
4. For each move make 10 shots from both sides of the paint.

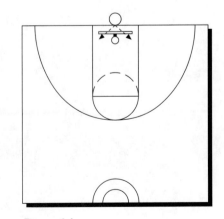

Figure 6.1

"Block my shot, please," pleads Rick Pitino (Louisville) to defender Eddie Griffin (Seton Hall, Houston Rockets). Pitino put hundreds of challengers in "jail," under the rim, but the only one who ever got him was the Miami Heat's Alonzo Mourning.

The Kevin McHale move on display during Orange-White playoff
action in August 2001.

Bill Aberer

LaSalle Academy
New York, New York

Low-Post Drills

Purpose: (1) To develop competency in shooting with both hands in the low-post area. (2) To improve jumping quickness. (3) To create good receiving position in the low-post area.

Figure 6.2

Drill 1: Mikan Drill (Figure 6.2)

1. Player 1 starts on left side of basket.
2. Make a crossover step to the other side and shoot a hook layup.
3. Let the ball bounce once and continuously do the same move on the other side.
4. Keys are to jump off one foot and shoot the ball back across your body.
5. Do three sets of 10 on each side.

Drill 2: Reverse Mikan Drill (Figure 6.3)

1. Same concept as in Drill 1.
2. Player 1 starts under the basket, facing the foul line.
3. Shoot reverse layups continuously.
4. Three sets of 10 on each side.

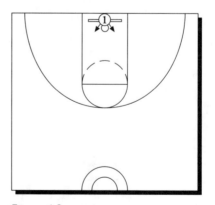

Figure 6.3

Drill 3: McHale Drill (Figure 6.4)

1. Player 1 uses one hand to tap ball off the bottom of the board so it comes back quickly.
2. You must quick jump.
3. The opposite hand touches the rim.
4. Repeat 10 on each side.

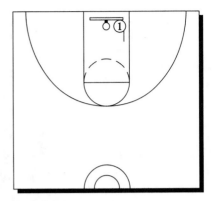

Figure 6.4

Drill 4: Dantley Drill (Figure 6.5)

1. Player 1 starts by throwing ball off the backboard from the foul line.
2. Rebound and bang ball off backboard in the air, come down, and go back up for a shot.
3. Repeat 10 on each side.

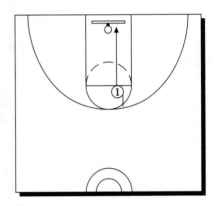

Figure 6.5

Drill 5: Walton Move (Figure 6.6)

1. Player 1 approaches the low block and gets position by putting his head in the defender's chest.
2. Player 1 stands facing the defender as the ball comes down the court.
3. When Player 2 is in position, sit and spin with your rear on the defender's thigh.
4. Player 1 receives the ball and executes a low-post move to score.

Figure 6.6

A pair of Five-Star head coaches (more than 40 years between them) rate among the finest big-man instructors in the game. Tom McCorry (shooting, left photo) demonstrates the Mikan Drill for Jason Collier (Georgia Tech, Houston Rockets) on the old RMU courts in 1995. LaSalle Academy's Bill Aberer (right photo) developed Ron Artest for St. John's and the Pacers and steered the Cardinals to an undefeated 27–0 CHSAA title in 1997. Aberer's venue is in the Frank Marino Memorial Fieldhouse in Honesdale in 1994.

Keith Holubesko

Five-Star Basketball Camp

Three C's Post Drill

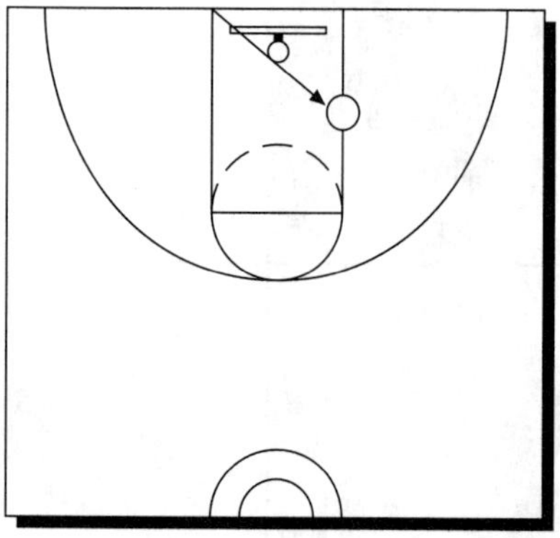

Figure 6.7

Purpose: This drill trains players to receive the basketball in the low post effectively.

Organization: Start on the baseline underneath a corner of the backboard with a basketball. The drill begins with the player spinning out a pass so that it is possible to receive the ball straddling the opposite first marker (Figure 6.7). When catching the ball, keep in mind the phrase, "Ball in the air, feet in the air." This allows the player to land on a jump-stop. The jump-stop increases balance and also gives a player the choice of a pivot foot. While receiving the ball, be sure to execute the three C's: catch, chin, and check).

★ *Catch*: Catch in twos (two eyes, two hands, two feet). Remember to call for the ball.
★ *Chin*: While catching the ball, bring it to the chin with both elbows up. This protects the ball and creates space for the post player.
★ *Check*: Once the ball is received, the post player must check for the defense by turning his head to the middle of the paint. (Feeling for pressure in a game also works.)

Players should execute this drill repeatedly by alternating sides. The goal is to land on balance consistently so that an effective offensive move may follow.

Following are three offensive low-post moves to use after mastering the three C's. All moves are completed from the three-C position.

The Drop-Step (Moses Malone)

When defense plays on the topside/middle, then drop-step baseline side.

1. Bring baseline foot to the basket.
2. Execute a low two-handed power dribble.
3. Land on a jump-stop with both shoulders parallel to the backboard and score.
4. Always use principle of "ball-you-man" to protect the ball from defense.
5. If defense beats you to the spot, spin dribble away and score.

The Jump-Hook (Kevin McHale)

1. Execute one power dribble to the middle and land on a jump-stop so that your shoulders are perpendicular to the basket (facing sideline).
2. Point inside elbow to basket while the ball is beside your opposite chin.
3. When shooting, jump into the defense slightly.
4. If defense defends the middle well, then execute a spin dribble to the baseline with the same hand.

The Up-and-Under (Dominique Wilkins)

Another great counter off the jump-hook.

1. Again, take the one power dribble to the middle.
2. Fake the jump shot and rip the ball across your body.
3. While using your same pivot foot, cross-step through and score.

The Walker Reverse Pivot

When bumped off the low-post area, use the reverse pivot to create space. Step back with your baseline foot and sweep the ball low to the middle side. Now you have the defense at your mercy. If the defender has hands low, shoot. If hands are high, shot-fake and drive. If cut off, then execute a spin dribble.

Make 10 from each spot on both sides of the basket.

Coach Keith Holubesko defends against a forthcoming drop-step.

Post Catch and Finish Drill

Alan Henderson

Atlanta Hawks

Purpose: To develop catching pass, keeping it high and finishing around the basket.

Hands-Up Drill (Figure 6.8)

1. Coach has the ball under the basket.
2. Player 1 starts halfway up the lane and works his way back and forth across the lane.
3. Keeping his hands high, Player 1 receives pass from coach and explodes to the basket, finishing with either hand.

Variation: can use reverse layup and backboard.

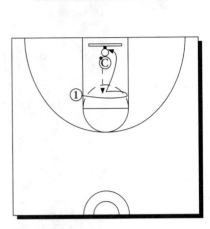

Figure 6.8

It's payback time! Alan Henderson (Brebuf High School) receives some cerebral pivot play instruction from then–Kentucky coach Rick Pitino in July 1990. Henderson copped Most Outstanding Player and Mr. Station 13 for a talent-laden Pitt II Five-Star session at RMU.

In 2000, after a stellar career at Indiana and for the Atlanta Hawks, Alan Henderson prepares campers for his "Block-to-Block" post moves series.

Four-Spot Shooting for Post Players

James "Bruiser" Flint

Drexel University
Philadelphia

Purpose: To develop low-post shooting from the baseline and elbow areas.

4-Spot Shooting Drill for Post Players (Figure 6.9)

1. Player X starts on baseline and makes the following moves.
2. Left short corner to left elbow, left elbow to right elbow, right elbow to right short corner
3. Coach passes to Player X from top of key.
4. Player X must make 10 shots before rotating to the next spot.

Variation: after 40 shots have been made, repeat the drill but use shot fake, one dribble jump shot.

Figure 6.9

Mike Fratello

NBA Analyst, TNT Network

Low-Post Double-Team Avoidance

Purpose: To develop the proper low-post footwork when avoiding the double team.

Figure 6.10

Drill 1: Catch and Go (Split—Figure 6.10)

1. Player 2 passes to Player 1 in the low post.
2. Player 1 catches the ball against X1.
3. X2 comes from the top-middle (free-throw line) to double team.
4. Player 1 immediately drop-steps to middle, splitting the trap before Player 2 gets set to block.
5. Player 1 finishes with strong middle jump shot or on other side of basket.

Drill 2: Spin Move (Figure 6.11)

1. Begin the same as Drill 1.
2. As X2 comes to double team, Player 1 now utilizes a spin move to the baseline to free up space.
3. Player 1 finishes with a baseline jump shot.

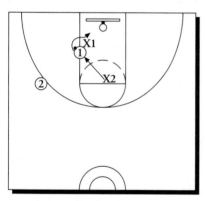

Figure 6.11

Drill 3: Dribble-Out Move (Figure 6.12)

1. Player 1 catches the ball in low post as in Drill 1.
2. But as X2 comes to double team, Player 1 takes two hard dribbles out to the perimeter to make a pass to Player 2.
3. Player 2 reverses the ball to Player 3 on opposite side.

Figure 6.12

Drill 4: Pass, Flash, and Repost
(Figure 6.13)

1. Player 1 catches pass in low post from Player 3.
2. X2 comes middle for double team.
3. Player 1 immediately pivots on high foot and passes to Player 2 on the opposite wing.
4. After Player 1 passes to Player 2, Player 1 immediately flashes to opposite low block area and reposts.

Figure 6.13

Drill 5: Steppin' Out
(David Robinson—Figure. 6.14)

1. Player 1 sets up as he did in Drills 1 through 4.
2. But now Player 1 pops out past the three-point line and becomes a perimeter passer.
3. Player 2 passes to Player 1 outside the three-point line.
4. Player 3 flashes middle from opposite wing flashing and receives a pass from Player 1.
5. Player 3 finishes with a jump shot or drive to the basket.

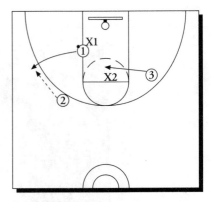

Figure 6.14

Post Screening: Baseline Series

Purpose: To develop proper screening techniques and footwork when screening on the baseline.

Drill 1: Drop-Foot Baseline
(Figure 6.15)

1. Player 2 starts on left side opposite of Player 1.
2. Player 1 sets a screen (at the first block marker) for Player 2 coming across the lane to the right wing.

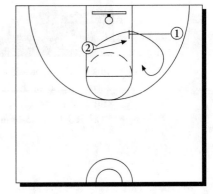

Figure 6.15

3. Player 1 immediately pulls right foot back so he is facing the baseline, which blocks the defender even more.

4. Player 1 can then turn and seal for a pass.

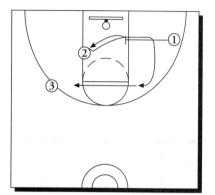

Figure 6.16

Drill 2: Reversal (2) (Figure 6.16)

1. Continuation of Drill 1. When Player 2 receives pass, he reverses the ball to Player 3 on opposite (left) wing.

2. Player 1 now pivots back (as he was when he set the screen) and steps up for a lob or flash to middle.

3. Player 3 passes to Player 1 for a post move.

Stay in school, pleads Mike Fratello, former coach of the Cavaliers and Hawks and TNT's current "Czar of the Telestrator." Fratello's audience included some of the top high school talent in the nation at RMU in July 2001. Fratello's math whittled the million bucks down to $121,500. It's a no-brainer, folks: Stay in school!

Back-to-Basket Moves

Jeff Ruland

Iona College
New Rochelle, New York

Purpose: To perform all of the back-to-the-basket moves (drop-step, up-and-under, baby, and turn-around jumper) under game-like conditions.

1. Place two basketballs on either side of the lane on the marker above the block (Figure 6.17).
2. Start in the paint with your back to the basket. Grab one basketball with two hands and do the drop-step move.
3. While your partner rebounds and replaces the ball, you grab the other ball and perform the drop-step move. Make sure that you properly position yourself before you start.
4. Continue until you make 10 baskets.

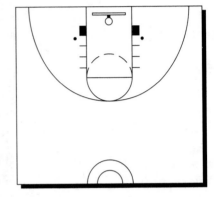

Figure 6.17

Perform each different post move in the same fashion.

A variation of the drill is to add a defender. While the second player rebounds and places the ball, a third player can play defense until the first player makes 10 baskets. You may also have two players battle for every rebound, whether it is a make or miss, and play from there.

Jeff Ruland in his Sixers body in overtime at Station 13

A trio of all-time Five-Star greats team up to deliver some heavy pivot play teaching at Radford in July 1985. Posting up is Lloyd Daniels (Nets), the top-rated high school junior in the country at the time. J. R. Reid (Cavs), the number-one senior prospect in the nation and MOP for the session prior to his All-American days at North Carolina, is the post defender. The teacher is Jeff Ruland, two-time All-NBA center (1984 and 1985) of the Washington Bullets, who returned to coach his alma mater, Iona, in 1988. Ruland, a Five-Star MOP himself in July 1976, shot a sparkling 56.4 percent from the field during his eight-year NBA career and was inducted into the Five-Star Hall of Fame in the summer of 2002.

Pete Gillen

University of Virginia
Charlottesville, Virginia

Secrets of Post Play

Purpose: To get the ball into the post.

1. Start opposite.
    * High to go low
    * Low to go high
    * Short steps first; then long steps
2. Land in two-foot jump-stop above box. Backboard can be best friend; don't want it to help defend.
3. Locate defense early.
    * Get contact and keep contact.
    * Go to defense.
    * Use body as weapon.
4. Give target hand away from defense.
5. Feel threatened—take step to meet ball.
    * When in doubt, move for ball.
    * Yes, lose prime position, but don't want to turn over ball.
    * Possession is most important.
6. Don't be afraid to kick it back out.
7. Can't be afraid to throw it inside.
8. Where is defense playing? Front, behind, 3/4 high side, 3/4 low side.
9. Must find angle for pass. Basketball is game of angles and percentages.
10. Look for target of pass.

Getting Fronted

1. Jump back into lane from defender. Now defender must turn head to find you, fake high to low and low to high.
2. Spin and pin.
    * Right foot between legs, spin right
    * Left foot between legs, spin left
3. Walk him up lane to create space for pass. Don't push off with hands, but bump his hips.

Pass to Fronted

1. Throw ball to corner of backboard.
2. Big man must release when ball is directly overhead.
3. Must fake pass.
    ★ Fake defender on post as well as on me.
    ★ Fake low, high.
    ★ Bring down, flip by ear (Bill Bradley).
    ★ Reverse pivot after fake low. Use body as a weapon.
4. Dribble to corner, start to take out, turn back to corner for flip pass.
5. Don't stand after pass.
    ★ Keep double down honest or burn him.
    ★ Stay behind 3-point line for spacing.
6. Laker cut
    ★ Feed post, cut to basket.
    ★ Prefer bounce pass into low post.
    ★ Big man defender doesn't want to get down and low.
    ★ Will prefer to go for block then make extra effort.

Drill 1: Two-on-Two Working on All of the Above

Drill 2: Three-on-Three Working on All of the Above

1. Add Sikma big-man pivot pass.
2. Step through triple down for pivot to go opposite.

Drill 3: Three-on-Three with Wing Moving

Opposite wing take man down low to block then high for triangle—high-low power.

Drill 4: Three-on-Three with Cut and Screen

1. Wait for screen and set him up.
2. Fake, then shoulder to shoulder.
   - ★ Pop for jumper at 45 degrees.
   - ★ Curl off screen. Look for tight play.
   - ★ Back-door cut to burn overplay. Look for overplay; fake and fade.
   - ★ Fade to corner for jumper. Look for defender sag; fake and fade.

Feed the Post

1. First whistle to second whistle
   - ★ Passer: defender
   - ★ Post: defender
   - ★ Block-to-block cut
   - ★ Defense doubles down
2. Triangle
   - ★ Passer: defender
   - ★ Wing: defender
   - ★ Post: defender
   - ★ Point dribble to wing
   - ★ Wing V-cuts to key
   - ★ Post block-to-block

7 keys for big guys

1. Fake high—go low.
2. Fake low—go high.
   - ★ Start opposite
   - ★ Short step, long step
3. Jump-stop—use both pivots.
4. Catch above block, locate defense.
5. Show target—away from defense.
6. Break defender arm—up or down.
7. Meet the ball.

Guards

1. Don't be afraid to throw it in.
2. Where is defense? Most play on high side.

3. Know angles.
    ★ High side, take to baseline
    ★ Low side, take to top
4. Look for target hand.
5. Fake pass.
    ★ Low: short violent fake, throw high
    ★ Low: reverse pivot
6. Pass in: spot up or Laker cut.
7. Second look

With ball in hand, Jeff Lebo (center) and Billy King (left) check out drillmaster Pete Gillen's exaggerated first step at Station 13 in July 1982. Lebo, a rising sophomore star at the time, went on to win a pair of Five-Star MOPs in 1984, earned All-America and All-ACC honors for Carlisle High School and North Carolina, respectively, and went on to the take the reins at Tennessee-Chattanooga in 2002. King was "Mr. Defense" at Five-Star and Duke and is now the general manager for the Philadelphia 76ers.

7

Shooting

Scott Wissel

Sacramento Kings
Memphis Grizzlies

Superstar Drill

Purpose: To work on eight basic but effective shooting moves off the dribble in order to better execute them in games. The drill is called the "superstar drill" not because the moves are flashy, but because the best shooters in the professional game are able to execute these moves on balance and under control. Quite simply, they are fundamental moves of the highest order.

Description: Eight cones will be placed around the perimeter of the basket (Figure 7.1). Player will begin at half-court. At each cone, a different move will be executed off the dribble. After each shot attempt, player will rebound the ball, then speed dribble back to half-court before attempting the next move. Player cannot move to the next cone until making shot at the previous cone. Drill concludes at half-court after one shot is made at each cone.

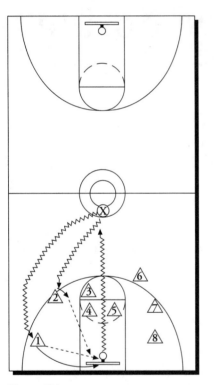

Figure 7.1

1. Pull-up J: Dribble directly to Cone 1 and shoot a straight pull-up jump shot.
2. Shot fake and step through: Dribble to Cone 2, shot fake, step by cone, and shoot.
3. Step back jump shot: Dribble to Cone 3, pull back one dribble and shoot the J.
4. Righty runner: Dribble to Cone 4 and shoot a right-handed runner in the lane.
5. Lefty runner: Dribble to Cone 5 and shoot the left-handed runner in the lane.
6. 3-point pull-up: Speed dribble to Cone 6 and shoot a 3-point shot.
7. Spin dribble into jumper: Speed dribble to Cone 7, spin back to the middle, and shoot.
8. Half-spin into pull-up J: Speed dribble to Cone 8, half-spin (fake-reverse), and shoot.

Points of emphasis

★ Execute each move at game speed but under control.

★ Pick the ball up off the dribble just above the shooting side knee with shooting on top of and in the center of the ball.
★ Follow through on each shot! Jump straight up and land on balance!
★ Drill may also be executed by doing the same move at each of the eight cones. (If shooting the runner, move the cones in, if shooting a 3, move the cones out.)

Six Spot Shootout

Objective: To practice shooting with precision; to build confidence and stamina.

Description: This drill involves one player (Figure 7.2). Player 1 starts in one corner. He or she must shoot and make the jump shot behind the cone before advancing to the next cone. The player will rebound his or her own shot and dribble back to the cone before shooting the ball. Once the player has made the shot behind each of the six cones, he or she must dribble back to the starting cone. This drill is done to improve time. A coach or teammate may time the drill with a stopwatch, or the individual player may use his or her own wristwatch. A good starting objective would be to make six shots within one minute. Remember that the player cannot advance to the next cone until he or she has made the shot at the previous cone.

Figure 7.2

This drill may also be executed with two players (Figure 7.3) or with as many as six players (Figure 7.4). Players must move in only one direction during the drill (i.e., clockwise), and they are not allowed to purposely interfere with another player's shot attempt. If two players arrive at the same cone at the same time, one doesn't have to wait for the other to shoot. As long as a shooter is behind the cone, he or she may shoot the ball as soon as possible.

Figure 7.3

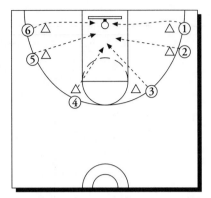

Figure 7.4

Teaching Points

★ Player should concentrate on maintaining proper form on each shot and holding the follow-through until the ball reaches the basket.

★ Player should hustle after each rebound, and speed dribble back to each cone.

★ Player should pick the ball up off the dribble just above the knee with the shooting hand on top of and in the center of the ball, then spring straight up and release the ball at the top of the jump.

★ Cones should be placed at equidistant spots around the basket (i.e., begin from 15 feet then move to the college three-point line, NBA three-point line, etc.).

★ Players should not rush the shot, and in spite of fatigue later in the drill, should concentrate on form and follow through!

Ironman Shooting

Objective: To practice shooting off the dribble; to develop stamina.

Description: Player utilizes all six baskets in the gym (Figure 7.5). Starting from center court, he or she dribbles to one basket and shoots a pull-up jump shot off the dribble from behind the foul line at that basket. On a miss, player will rebound the ball and dribble back to free-throw line at that basket and shoot again until shot is made. On a make, he or she will rebound the ball and speed dribble to the next basket and execute the same shot. Once a jump shot is made at each of the six baskets, the player speeds back to center court and the clock (stopwatch) stops.

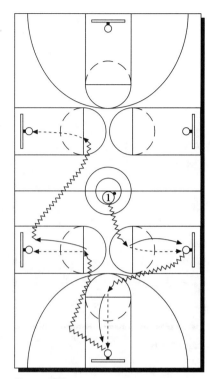

Teaching Points

★ This drill should be done for time (i.e., how fast a player can make six pull-up jump shots). Another option is to run the drill for a set of minutes (i.e., one minute, two minutes, five minutes, etc.) and see how many jump shots the player can make.

★ Player should concentrate on utilizing good dribbling form (head up, waist high dribble) and maintaining proper shooting form. Hold the follow-through until the ball goes into the basket before following the shot. Jump and land on balance.

Figure 7.5

★ This drill also may be done with more than one player and with as many as 12 (coach may start drill with two players at a basket).

At the Five-Star session in Honesdale, Pa., we do this drill utilizing all 20 outdoor baskets, and the all-time record stands at 3:38—three minutes, thirty-eight seconds—for 20 baskets made off the dribble from behind the free-throw line.

Bill Bradley Shooting Drill/Workout

Objective: To develop consistency, accuracy, and confidence in shooting.

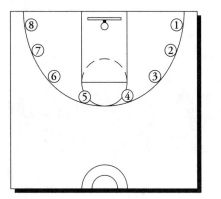

Figure 7.6

Description: Player chooses eight spots on the perimeter to shoot from (Figure 7.6). Player begins by attempting to make a set number of jump shots in a row before moving on to the next spot. In Bradley's case, he would try to make 10 out of 13 jump shots from one spot before moving on to the next. Or, to make the workout more challenging, he would make 10 in a row from each spot before moving on to the next. He was such a disciplined and accurate shooter that it was often said, "People would pay just to watch him warm up!"

Teaching Points

★ Player should concentrate on good shooting form. Hold the follow-through up on every shot. Jump and land in the same spot, on balance. Shoot with confidence.

★ Player should shoot game-condition type shots. Many players tend to shoot lazy jump shots when they are practicing on their own. But the determined player takes each practice shot as if it were in a game.

★ To make the drill more rewarding, player should hustle after the rebound and toss the ball back to the spot, jump behind the ball, and catch the ball high in front of the shooting-side shoulder before going straight up into the shot and releasing the ball with proper form.

Scott Wissel demonstrates the "Superstar" Drill with 2002 NBA All-Star and Dream Team member Elton Brand at Honesdale in August 1996.

The early bird gets the worm. Scott Wissel (Sacramento Kings) demonstrating proper preparation for the hook shot at 7:00 a.m. optional "Redeye" at Honesdale in August 1999.

Scott Wissel (center, with ball) has just broken his own Shooting Marathon record, setting a new mark of 2 hours and 51 minutes at Bryn Mawr in August 2002. Of course, they were all late for dinner.

Three-Point Shooting Drills

Bob Leckie

Saint Peter's College
Jersey City, New Jersey

Objective: Nothing has changed the game of basketball in America more than the advent of the three-point shot. It has become an effective tool in every team's arsenal, whether used as a prominent part of an offensive philosophy or as a strategy for making a comeback late in the game. Mathematics tells us that a team shooting 35 percent from three-point territory is actually better than one shooting 50 percent from two-point land. With this in mind, I would like to present the following three-point shooting drills.

Drill 1: Bang-Bang

We use this terminology because we like our players to understand that their ball reversal should take no longer than for us to say the words "Bang bang." This emphasizes the quickness of their passes in order to get the ball to the open shooter. The drill starts with the ball in Player 1's hands and his teammates lined up in their respective lines.

1. Player 1 pass fakes to an imaginary post man and then throws a sharp two-handed overhead pass to Player 3 (Figure 7.7).
2. Player 3 then reverses the ball with a two-handed chest pass to Player 5, who is spotted up with his inside pivot foot, in this case, his right foot, planted behind the three-point line with his hands ready to catch the ball ("spotting up").
3. After Player 5 catches the ball he pivots into his shot (Figure 7.8). He rebounds his own shot and passes it to the next player in Player 1's line.
4. Players rotate counterclockwise to the line that they passed (Figure 7.9).

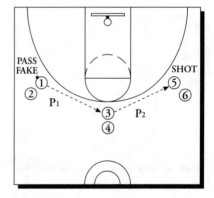

Figure 7.7

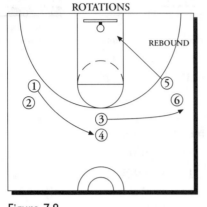

Figure 7.8

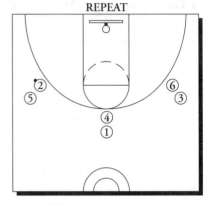

Figure 7.9

The drill proceeds for the next players in line. Players can shoot until a set number of shots are made; I like 10 made shots. The drill then reverses itself in the opposite direction so that the players on the left side of the court take the shots on a clockwise rotation.

Drill 2: One-More

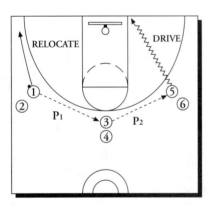

Figure 7.10

1. This drill is set up as illustrated with three lines (two at wings and one at point). We again make use of the pass fake into the imaginary post man and ball reversal to the opposite side of the court. This time, however, we drive baseline (Figure 7.10) and throw a pass to the opposite side guard who relocates and is spotted up for the shot in the opposite corner (Figure 7.11).

2. The player in the corner then makes another pass to the player in the middle who had relocated and shoots after he receives the ball—hence the name "one-more" (Figure 7.12). Players must communicate by calling for the ball by saying "one more."

Figure 7.11

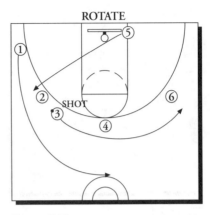

Figure 7.12

Drill 3: Penetrate-and-Kick

1. Once again, this drill is set up as illustrated with the players in their respective lines. We continue to use the pass fake to the post area and the ball reversal passing technique to reinforce these good habits (Figure 7.13).
2. Once the ball is reversed from one side to the other, the player penetrates to the middle by using the dribble and kicks it out to the player spotted up outside the three-point line (Figure 7.14).
3. The rotation is clockwise with the penetrater rebounding the ball and going to the end of the shooting line (Figure 7.15).

Drill 4: Kick-and-Pass

This drill is the same as the "penetrate and kick" drill but with an extra pass to the players in the middle line for the shot (Figures 7.16 and 7.17). Player rotations remain the same (Figure 7.18).

Throughout these drills we teach the pass fake, the overhead pass, two-handed chest pass, spotting up, 1-2 step, ball reversal, and communication along with baseline drive and dribble penetration. As we get more proficient at these drills, we add cones or managers to act like defensive men.

Figure 7.13

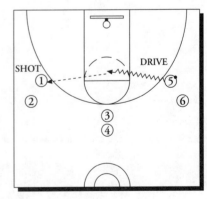

Figure 7.14

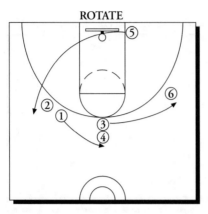

Figure 7.15

Figure 7.16

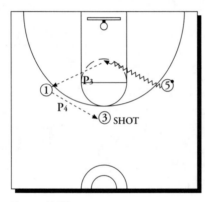

Figure 7.17

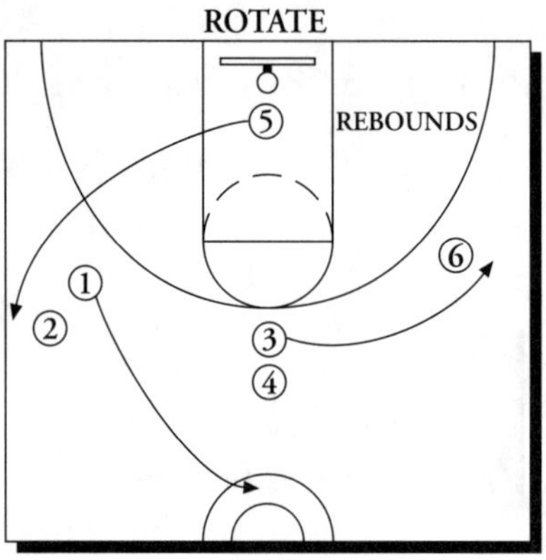

Figure 7.18

Curl-and-Fade Drill

Hubie Brown

Memphis Grizzlies

Purpose: To learn how to read the defense and develop shooting while coming off a screen.

Drill 1: Curl and Fade (Figure 7.19)

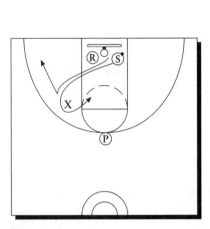

★ P is the passer at the top of key.
★ R is the rebounder who will outlet to passer after each shot.
★ X is the screener.
★ S will come off screens using the curl and fade.
★ Catch ball in a "T," ready to shoot and get behind it.
★ Come under the basket each time.
★ Drill is done on both sides.

Figure 7.19

Pictures don't always tell a thousand words. Award-winning broadcaster Hubie Brown appears to be on the air for TNT, but the microphone is courtesy of *One Love*, a forthcoming hoop documentary produced by Disney and filmed in part at Five-Star in July 1999. Northwestern's Jitim Young is about to attack Brown's closeout.

Barry Brodzinski

Paul VI High School
Haddonfield, New Jersey

Two-Spot Drill

Objective: This actually involves eight drills that can be done off two spots at the foul line extended on both wings (Figure 7.20). The drills develop both hands and footwork going in four different directions. This drill should be done at full speed, as hard as possible.

1. *Shoot off speed dribble:* five shots each direction, both sides.
2. *Shoot off self pass:* five shots each direction, both sides.
3. *Jab-step shot:* shoot off the jab-step going directly into the shot using both feet. Five shots each, both sides.
4. *Quick shot:* jab, plus one dribble. Five shots each direction, both sides.
5. *Space-maker move:* jab, plus one dribble, plus wide crossover. Five shots each direction, both sides.
6. *Between legs into shot:* five shots each direction, both sides.
7. *Behind-the-back dribble into shot:* five shots each direction, both sides.
8. *Conditioning shooting drill:* put ball on ground. Run and touch the baseline, then come back and pick the ball up and shoot. Rebound your shot. Dribble and put the ball down in the original spot and repeat. Go hard for 10 shots and do the same thing on the opposite wing.

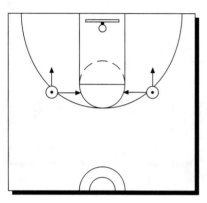

Figure 7.20

Triangle-Shooting Drill (Figure 7.21)

1. Start under the basket. Dribble out left-handed above three-point line, turn crossover back inside 15-foot range and shoot.

2. Rebound your own shot and then dribble out right-handed in opposite direction above the three-point line.
3. Crossover back to 15 foot range and shoot.
4. Continue doing this each direction until 10 shots are made; then repeat.

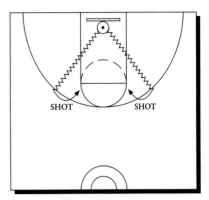

Figure 7.21

Beat-the-Ghost

This is a great spot-shooting drill. Begin by making a foul shot. Then play against yourself or the ghost (Figure 7.22).

★ You must make 21 shots before you miss seven.
★ Each made shot counts as one point and each miss counts as three points. You cannot make two shots in a row from the same spot.
★ If, initially, you lose to the ghost, continue through until you make 21 shots no matter how many you missed. This will let you see your improvement and let you know what you need to do to beat the ghost!
★ This can be all 15-foot shots or all three-point shots, but it should not be a combination.

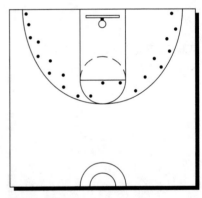

Figure 7.22

Circus-Shooting Drill

This appears to be an easy drill as you are attempting to make five shots from five spots (Figure 7.23). However, it is an extremely difficult drill as you are under pressure to push yourself to make all these shots in under 20 seconds!

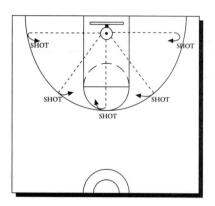

Figure 7.23

1. Start under the basket and throw a self-pass to the corner. Catch and turn, take one dribble, and shoot.
2. After the shot, rebound and throw to the opposite corner. Repeat.
3. Rebound and throw to opposite wing, rebound, and throw to the other wing.
4. Rebound and throw to top of key.

You must make four shots to stop; otherwise, continue repeating the drill until you get them.

Shooting Series

Purpose: To develop shooting skills while utilizing minimal dribbles.

Drill 1: Two-Dribble Extension (Figure 7.24)

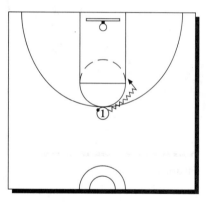

Figure 7.24

1. Player 1 takes two hard dribbles toward foul line extended.
2. Player 1 pulls up for a foul-line jump shot.
3. Must be just inside the elbow for a jump shot.

Drill 2: Two-Dribble Backup/Crossover (Figure 7.25)

1. Player 1 starts at baseline and passes to Player 2 coming from half-court, catching at the free-throw line extended.
2. Player 2 waits for Player 1 to come around him and play defense.
3. Player 2 takes two dribbles right, then two back-up dribbles back, a crossover dribble, and finishes going hard to half-court.
4. Switch and repeat.

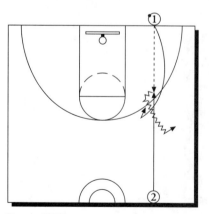

Figure 7.25

Drill 3: Defeating the Three-Point Line (Figure 7.26)

1. Player 1 catches pass from Player 2 at the three-point line.
2. Player 1 takes one hard dribble inside the three-point line and goes to the basket.
3. Repeat, but instead pull up for a 15-foot jump shot.

Drill 4: Using the Three-Point Line (Figure 7.27)

1. Player 1 passes to Player 2 at the three-point line.
2. Player 2 stops and pulls up for a jump shot.
3. Focus on footwork, so you land outside the three-point line, not on it or inside it.
4. Repeat, but use a jab-step and pull-back jump shot.

Figure 7.26

Figure 7.27

Barry Brodzinski (Paul VI High School, Haddonfield, N.J.), a former LaSalle College star and the man who guided Roman Catholic High School to a pair of Catholic League crowns, scores from long distance at his sold-out guard camp in July 2001. His shooting drills have been a mainstay of the Five-Star backcourt camp for years.

Rick Pitino

University of Louisville
Louisville, Kentucky

Billy Donovan Shooting Drill

Purpose: To practice shooting under game-like conditions.

Organization: Two players are needed (Figure 7.28): one starts under the basket with a basketball; the other starts in a corner in a ready-to-catch position (low and hands in front). The drill begins with the player in the corner moving forward while calling for the ball. The player under the basket delivers a chest pass and then runs with one hand up toward the other player and yells, "Shot!" He is not attempting to block the shot but give the shooter a realistic feel for the time he has to shoot. The shooter gets his rebound and replaces his partner under the basket. The passer becomes the shooter. The drill can be done at five spots on the court (corners, wings, and point). Shoot at each spot for 30 seconds. A second round can take place, but this time add a shot fake, one dribble (body to body), and then a jump shot.

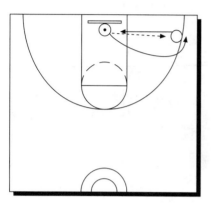

Figure 7.28

Ultimate Shooting Series

Purpose: To develop shooting skills off the catch and dribble and with the use of the jab-step and shot fake.

Drill 1: 1-2 Step Catch and Shoot (Figure 7.29)

★ Player 1 flashes from left corner to the right elbow for a pass from Player 2 on right wing.
★ Player 1 catches with a 1-2 step and immediately shoots.

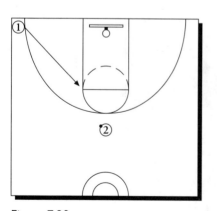

Figure 7.29

Variation: repeat drill but catch 1-2 and then jab step and drive to basket.

Variation: repeat drill but catch 1-2 and then shot fake and shoot.

Drill 2: Block Pivot and Shoot (Figure 7.30)

★ Player 1 flashes from weak-side baseline to strong-side block (first marker).
★ Player 1 receives the pass from Player 2, front pivots toward basket, and shoots.

Variation: repeat drill, but jab step and then drive to basket.

Variation: repeat drill, but then shot-fake and shoot.

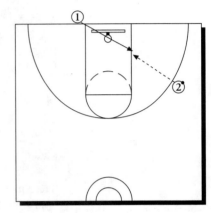

Figure 7.30

Drill 3: Baseline Moves (Figure 7.31)

1. Player 2 starts with ball under basket and passes to Player 1.
2. Player 1 starts in the left corner and catches pass from Player 2 in a 1-2 step.
3. Player 2 stunts out at Player 1 and plays defense.
4. Player 2 uses jab-step series and moves off one dribble.

Figure 7.31

Rick Pitino will go anywhere to teach! Here he uses the stands of the Gus Krop gym at RMC to make a teaching point during a lecture in July 1987. Pitino was head coach of the Knicks at the time.

Over 100 NBA pros have graduated from Five-Star's rising sophomore development league, but none with more flair than Lebron James (St. Vincent-Mary in Akron, Ohio). Moving up to the NBA division mid-week of the Pitt III, 2000 session, and playing in both leagues, James became the only camper in the 37-year history of Five-Star to play in two Orange-White All-Star classics in the same week and garnered MVP of the DL contest. Here he walks onto the national stage for the first time as a demonstrator for then–Celtics coach Rick Pitino's "Ultimate Shooting Series."

Perimeter Shooting Series

Mike Dunleavy

NBA Analyst

Purpose: To develop perimeter shooting with use of the jab-step and a rip-through move

Drill 1: 125 Inside/Outside Shots (Figure 7.32)

★ Using five spots around the perimeter (left corner, left wing, top of key, right wing, and right corner), shoot 25 shots from each spot.
★ Repeat drill inside the three-point line and then outside the three-point line.
★ Shoot 100 free throws after each set.

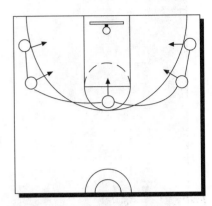

Figure 7.32

Drill 2: Jab-Step 125 Inside/Outside Shots (Figure 7.33)

★ Same as Drill 1, but use the jab-step, one dribble to create space for shot.
★ Inside and outside the three-point line
★ Shoot 100 free throws after each set.

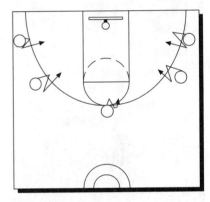

Drill 3: 125 Rip Through Inside/Outside Shots (Figure 7.34)

★ Same as Drill 1, but use the rip-through move in which you catch the ball and rip it below your knees as you take 1-2 dribbles to create space for shot.
★ Inside and outside the three-point line
★ Shoot 100 free throws after each set.

Figure 7.33

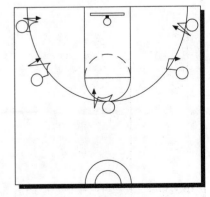

Figure 7.34

Triple-three Mike Dunleavy Sr., teacher, coach, and still-great shooter, waves goodbye to his basketball at RMU in July 2000. He had winning records with the Blazers and Bucks, led the NBA in three-point marksmanship two years, shot a sparkling .467 in eleven seasons, and was inducted into the NYC Basketball Hall of Fame in September 2001.

Mike Dunleavy's jump-shooting form

Mike Krzyzewski

Duke University
Durham, North Carolina

Rapid-Fire Three-Point Shooting

Purpose: To develop three-point shooting fundamentals and techniques while on the move.

★ Players 1, 2, and 3 begin spread out beyond the three-point line with a ball.
★ Three rebounders start under the basket.
★ Each shooter must shoot continuous three-point shots for five minutes, moving to different spots.
★ Rebounders must pass to partner they started with.
★ Players 1, 2, and 3 must call for the ball and be ready to shoot.
★ Keep track of three-point shots made over five minutes from all three players.

Nobody on the collegiate scene uses the trifecta with more devastation on his opponents than Duke's Mike Krzyzewski. A trio of national championships (1991, 1992, 2001) were to follow Coach K's three-point shooting demonstration at Radford in 1989.

Layup-Elbow-Post Shooting Drill

James "Bruiser" Flint

Drexel University
Philadelphia

Purpose: To develop shooting from different spots on the floor.

Drill 1: Sprint to Layup
(Phase 1—Figure 7.35)

1. Players start at baseline corner.
2. Player sprints to same corner of half-court, makes a hard V-cut, and goes directly to the basket.
3. Coach at the top of the key passes to player, who must shoot layup without dribbling.
4. Player rebounds his shot and passes to other coach, in corner.

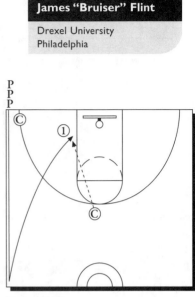

Figure 7.35

This drill can be varied by using different types of passes and shots as well as by changing the passing lanes.

Drill 2: Layup to Elbow
(Phase 2—Figure 7.36)

1. Player 1 rebounds own shot and passes out to coach at top of key.
2. Player 1 continues on to the opposite elbow for jump shot.
3. Follow any misses.
4. Player 1 continues on to Phase 3 of the drill.

Figure 7.36

Drill 3: Elbow to Post
(Phase 3—Figure 7.37)

1. Player 1 passes rebound out to coach in left corner after elbow jump shot.
2. Player 1 continues to dive to block.

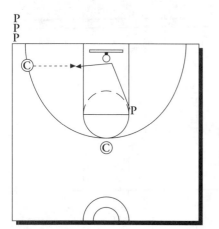

Figure 7.37

3. Player 1 receives pass from coach in left corner and executes a post move.
4. Follow any misses.
5. Players go twice each side.

60-Second Perimeter Shooting Drill

Purpose: To develop speed shooting from different perimeter spots.

★ Player 1 starts in corner with 60 seconds on the clock (Figure 7.38).
★ Player 1 has to make three shots from each X spot before rotating to the next.
★ Objective is to get from corner to corner in 60 seconds.

Variation: push clock to 90 seconds and move spots to outside the 3-point line.

Figure 7.38

Toss-Back Shooting Series

Mike Fratello

NBA Analyst, TNT Network

Purpose: To develop the proper perimeter shooting techniques off a pass.

Drill 1: Corner-Elbow Shots (Figure 7.39)

1. Player 1 starts in left corner and passes to coach at the top of key.
2. Player 1 follows the flight of the pass with hands ready to shoot.
3. Player 1 receives a pass back from coach at the ball-side elbow for a jump shot.

Figure 7.39

Drill 2: Top-Elbow Shots (Figure 7.40)

1. Player 1 starts at top of key and passes to coach in the corner.
2. Player 1 follows the flight of the pass with hands ready to shoot.
3. Player 1 receives a pass back from coach at the ball-side elbow for a jump shot.

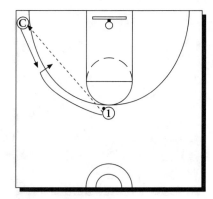

Figure 7.40

Drill 3: Elbow-Elbow Shots (Figure 7.41)

1. Player 1 starts at the left elbow and passes to coach at the right elbow.
2. Player 1 follows the flight of the pass with hands ready to shoot.
3. Player 1 receives a pass back from coach at the ball-side elbow for a jump shot.

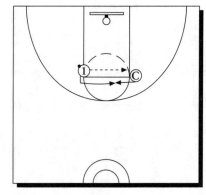

Figure 7.41

John Calipari

University of Memphis
Memphis, Tennessee

Tiger Shooting Series

Purpose: To develop the proper footwork for shooting when using a screen, pulling up, or after use of a dribble.

Drill 1: Big Strides (Figure 7.42)

1. Player 1 starts at ball-side baseline.
2. Taking "big strides," comes off an opposite block screen and sprints toward Coach 1.
3. Coach 1 passes to Player 1 at ball-side elbow for a catch and shot.

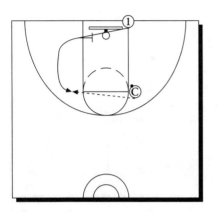

Figure 7.42

Drill 2: Two-Dribble Pull-Ups (Figure 7.43)

1. Player 1 and Player 2 start at opposite wings.
2. Both take two hard dribbles toward the free-throw line and pull up for a jump shot.
3. Repeat, but both players take two hard dribbles down the sideline and pull up for a baseline jump shot.
4. Turn into the shot!

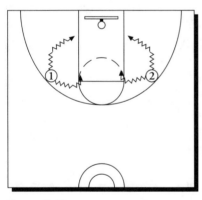

Figure 7.43

Drill 3: Transition Pull-Up (Figure 7.44)

1. Player 1 starts at half-court.
2. Taking two hard dribbles, he proceeds toward free-throw line.
3. At free-throw line, Player 1 pulls up for a jump shot.
4. Follow shot and repeat for 30 seconds, making as many shots as possible.

Figure 7.44

Drill 4: Combo Dribbling Moves (Figure 7.45)

1. Player 1 and Player 2 start at half-court on right and left sides.
2. Each player completes a behind-the-back dribble and a between-the-legs dribble with one dribble in between.
3. Both players pull up for a jump shot at the elbow.

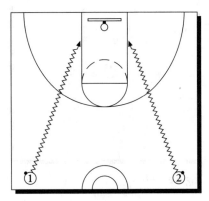

Figure 7.45

Drill 5: 7 Spot/10 in a Row (Figure 7.46)

★ Player 1 shoots from seven spots on the floor.
★ Try to make 10 in a row.
★ Only two misses allowed per turn.

Drill 6: 3 Shots/5 Spots/90 Seconds (Figure 7.47)

★ Using a rebounder (R) and passer (P), player begins at the spot marked "S" and must make three shots from each spot in 90 seconds.
★ Repeat drill, beginning at a different starting spot, but must make three *in a row* to move to next spot.

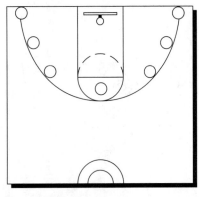

Figure 7.46

Drill 7: 3/2 Drill (Figure 7.48)

1. Start with three players and two basketballs.
2. Players 1 and 2 start with ball, while Player 3 sets up ready to shoot.
3. Player 1 shoots, follows his shot and gets his own rebound, then passes to Player 3, who has spotted up.

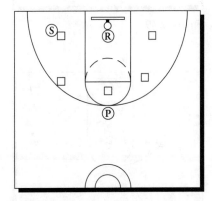

Figure 7.47

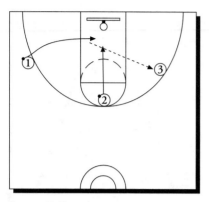

Figure 7.48

4. Player 2 shoots, grabs his own rebound, and now passes to Player 1, who has spotted up.
5. Player 3, after receiving the pass from Player 1, now shoots and grabs his own rebound, passing to Player 2, who has spotted up.

Pick-and-Roll Shooting Series

Purpose: To develop proper screening techniques and shooting off the screen.

Drill 1: Lob Drill (Figure 7.49)

Figure 7.49

1. Player 1 screens down for Player 2.
2. Player 2, taking "big steps," comes off screen and catches a pass from Coach A for jump shot.
3. Player 1, taking "big steps," goes toward basket for lob from Coach B.

Variation: Player 2 can curl up and Player 1 can screen, then hit elbow for jumper.

Drill 2: Pick-and-Roll and Receive Drill (Figure 7.50)

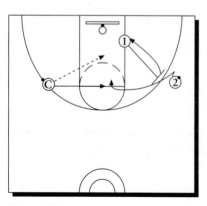

Figure 7.50

1. Player 2 starts with ball on wing.
2. Player 1 comes from ball-side block to set a ball screen for Player 2.
3. Player 1 rolls and receives a pass from coach (C).
4. Instead of passing to Player 1, coach can pass to Player 2, who can take an immediate jump shot at the free-throw line or make a hesitation move and drive to the basket.
5. Player 2 can also work on splitting the screen.

Shooting off the Dribble Series

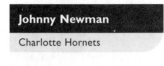
Johnny Newman
Charlotte Hornets

Purpose: To develop shooting off a series of dribble moves.

Drill 1: Inside/Out Move (Figure 7.51)

1. Player 1 dribbles up to coach at right elbow.
2. Player 1 uses an inside/out dribble move.
3. Player 1 takes an additional dribble to create space.
4. Player 1 then pulls up for a jump shot in middle lane extended area.
5. Repeat from left side.

Figure 7.51

Drill 2: Crossover Move (Figure 7.52)

1. Player 1 dribbles up to coach at right elbow.
2. Player 1 uses a crossover dribble from right to left.
3. Player 1 takes an additional dribble to create space.
4. Player 1 then pulls up for a jump shot in the middle of the lane area.
5. Repeat from left side.

Figure 7.52

Drill 3: Hesitation Move (Figure 7.53)

1. Player 1 dribbles up to coach at right elbow.
2. Player 1 uses a hesitation dribble.
3. Player 1 takes an additional dribble to create space.
4. Player 1 then pulls up for a jump shot in the middle of the lane extended area.
5. Repeat from left side.

Figure 7.53

Fifteen-year NBA pro and Five-Star stalwart as camper, counselor, and clinician, Johnny Newman holds court in Hampden-Sydney in June 2001. Newman was one of the NBA's most reliable clutch shooters and scorers.

Wolfpack Shooting

Herb Sendek

North Carolina State University
Raleigh, North Carolina

Objective: To beat the double team in the post-by-post entry and by relocating on the perimeter for the jump shot.

When you pass inside you must move. Make the defender find you and move farther. It's too easy to guard a stationary player. Be a moving target. Make the defender pay for doubling down. But remember, you must take what defense gives you.

Drill 1 (Figure 7.54)

1. Passer feeds post from wing (triple threat to bounce pass).
2. Post feeds wing who has faded to corner
   ★ Catch chest pass in triple threat ready to shoot
   ★ Shooter must get shoulder square ready to shoot
3. Post passer yells, "Shot!"
4. Shooter becomes post player.

Figure 7.54

Drill 2 (Figure 7.55)

1. Point passes to high post on elbow for rub and flip.
   ★ Man not open on first cutter
   ★ First cutter continues to low post
2. Wing V-cuts to overtop for flip and three pointer.
3. Square shoulder (pivot off inside, swing gate with outside)

Rotation on Drill

★ First cutter becomes wing
★ Second cutter becomes post
★ Post to end of line on point

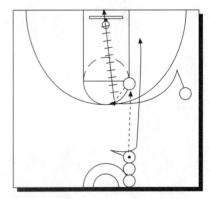

Figure 7.55

8

Transition Game

Kevin Pigott

Fordham Preparatory School
Bronx, New York

Transition Fast Break

Purpose: To develop offensive ball movement and defensive transition in both the half-court and full-court.

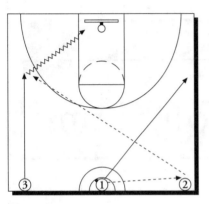

Figure 8.1

Drill 1: Three-on-None (Half-Court— Figure 8.1)

1. Player 1 starts at center court with ball.
2. Player 2 is on the right wing.
3. Player 3 is on the left wing.
4. Player 1 passes to Player 2 and sprints to the sideline that Player 2 caught the ball at.
5. Player 3 full sprints to the opposite sideline.
6. Player 2 now passes to Player 3 for layup shot.

Variation: if two defenders are added, limit offense to two dribbles and two passes. Start defenders on each sideline, foul-line extended.

Drill 2: Three-on-Three (Full-Court— Figure 8.2)

1. Players 1, 2, and 3 start lined up across the baseline.
2. X1, X2, and X3 line up across from each offense at free-throw line and extended.
3. Coach has the ball (anywhere) and passes to any offensive player.
4. The defender of the offensive player who receives the pass must run and touch the baseline.
5. Players 1, 2, and 3 run their fast break as the remaining two defenders get back in transition.

★ *Offensive Rules:* get the ball to the middle, to a ballhandler, and get up the floor (wide).

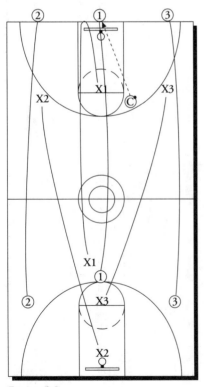

Figure 8.2

★ *Defensive Rules*: get back in transition to
protect basket and stop ball; trailing
defender must get back in open area.

Variation: can use point system on both ends, for
example:

★ Offensive scoring:
2-point FG
3-point FG
1 point for offensive rebound
1 point for nonshooting foul
★ Defensive scoring: rebound/stop/deflection
are each 1 point.
★ Air ball is 1 point.
★ Steal is 2 points.
★ Charge is 3 points.
★ Matchup is 1 point (e.g., three-on-two
becomes two-on-two because last defensive
player hustles back).

Bridgewater-Raritan head coach Tim Ortelli teaches "freedom from the press" as Cleveland
Cavalier Dajuan Wagner trails the ball.

Mike Fratello

NBA Analyst, TNT Network

Full-Court Defense Transition Drill

Purpose: To develop the proper defensive rotations when defending in a three-on-two transition.

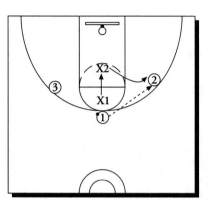

Figure 8.3

Drill: Three-on-Two Fast Break

1. Players 1, 2, and 3 begin a fast break up the floor focusing on keeping the ball in the middle and spreading the defense (Figure 8.3).
2. X1 and X2 run the middle of the no-further-than-lane width in defensive transition.
3. X2 gets back under the rim and works his way to the middle of the lane and protects the basket.
4. X1 gets back to the top of key to stop ball and force the pass to the wing (force left or right).
5. As Player 1 passes to Player 2 on the right wing, free-throw line extended, X2 must rotate and closeout to cover him.
6. X1 now drops to the lower part of the middle of the lane to protect the basket.
7. On the reversal pass from Player 2 to Player 1, X2 rotates over and closes out (Figure 8.4).
8. X1 can stunt to help but must stay at home to protect the basket.
9. If Player 2 skips the ball to Player 3 on the left wing, then X1 has to take the second pass (Figure 8.5).
10. Note: X2 takes first and second pass, except on a skip pass.

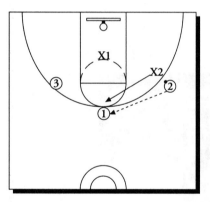

Figure 8.4

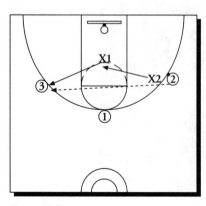

Figure 8.5

Full-Court "Press" Defensive Drills

Billy Donovan

University of Florida
Gainesville, Florida

Purpose: To develop the proper defensive rotations when pressing in the full court.

Drill 1: Press Build-Up (Two-on-One)

★ Trap on three occasions (Figure 8.6): (1) below the block (if in the coffin corner or reverse pivot), (2) uncontrolled speed dribble, (3) top of key.
★ X1 and X2 work together to trap Player 1 (Figure 8.7).
★ Only use Side A of the floor in this drill.
★ Look for steal off basketball.
★ X1 and X2 come together to trap Player 1 (Figure 8.8).
★ Always attack the offense.
★ X1 and X2 sprint out of trap (Figure 8.9).
★ X2 sprints in front of the basketball and keeps the ball on one side of the floor.
★ This allows X1 to "run through the basketball."
★ X2 keeps dribbler on one side of the floor, allowing X1 to "run through the basketball" (Figure 8.10).

Drill 2: Press Build-Up (Three-on-Three)

★ X1 guards the ball (Figure 8.11).
★ X2 and X3 switch on any screens that are set by Players 2 or 3.
★ Same trapping principles as two on one drill (Figure 8.12).
★ If Player 2 catches the ball, X1 drops back to the level of the ball.
★ X2 contains the dribbler.

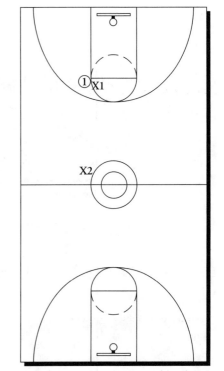

Figure 8.6

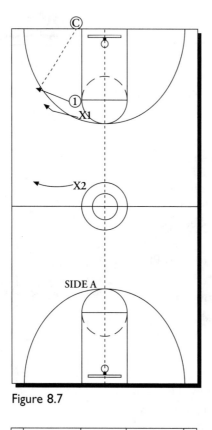

Figure 8.7

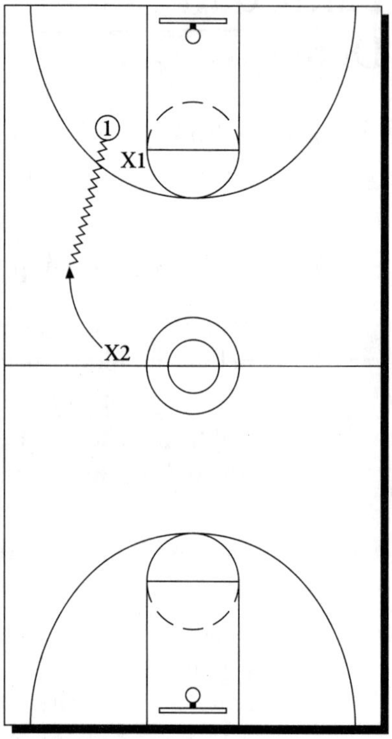

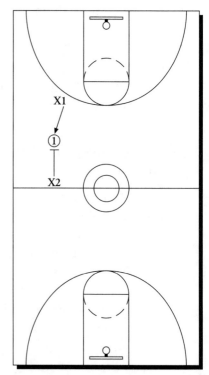

Figure 8.8

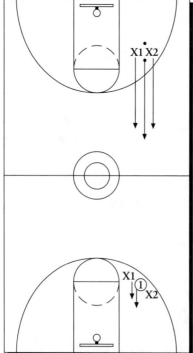

Figure 8.9

Figure 8.10

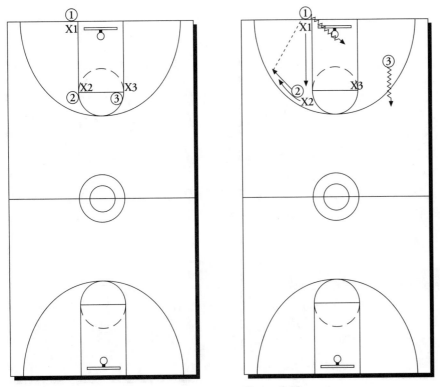

Figure 8.11   Figure 8.12

★ If X2 is beaten, X1 levels off the ball and
   X2 and X1 trap together (Figure 8.13).
★ Must mirror the basketball in the trap
★ If Player 2 passes to Player 1, X2 chases
   pass as X3 prepares to come up to trap.
★ X1 must sprint to cover middle.

Drill 3: Press Build-Up (Four-on-Four—Figures 8.14 and 8.15)

★ Four on four full-court with same trapping
   rules and principles.
★ Important to communicate
★ Back-tip the dribbler.
★ Mirror the basketball.
★ Sprint out of traps and "run through the
   basketball."

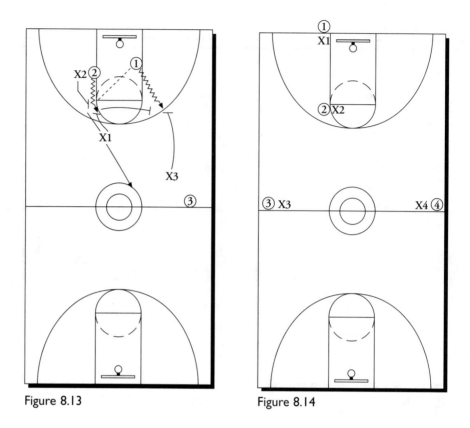

Figure 8.13   Figure 8.14

Drill 4: Press Build-Up (Five-on-Five— Figure 8.16)

★ Five-on-five full-court with same trapping rules and principles
★ Be aggressive in traps.
★ Don't let the offense come to you.
★ Attack the offense.

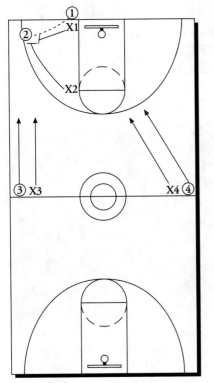

Figure 8.15

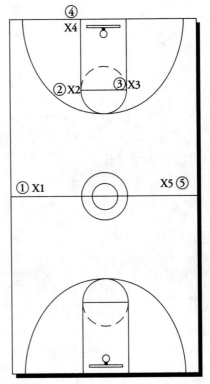

Figure 8.16

"Coachability" is the appropriate word for this apt pupil in Billy Donovan's one-on-one teaching maneuvers at Honesdale in August 2002. "Billy the Kid" graduated from this very same venue 20 years earlier to lead Providence to a miracle Final Four finish in 1987. He also played under Rick Pitino for the Knicks and coached the Florida Gators to four straight 20-win seasons, two consecutive SEC titles, and the 2000 Final Four. Donovan was inducted into the Providence College and Five-Star halls of fame in 2000 and 2002, respectively.

Five-Man Weave/Three-on-Two/Two-on-One

Bob Traina

Seminole High School
Sanford, Florida

Number of players needed: 10 players with two basketballs

Drill time needed: 4–8 minutes

Drill alignment: five lines, ball in middle

Defensive Concepts Taught

★ Conditioning and defensive transition
★ Stop dribble penetration and defensive communication
★ Contest shot and rebound

Offensive Concepts Taught

★ Offensive transition
★ Proper spacing
★ Shot selection—primary fast break

1. Five players must execute weave down court. Player 1 passes the ball two men away from himself and sprints around those two men. Play will continue until the fourth pass is made. The fourth pass is a *bounce* pass for a *layup*.
2. Passer and shooter will sprint back down court. The other three players will touch baseline and come back downcourt three-on-two, attacking with basic three-on-two fundamentals. Ball is pushed hard upcourt with long passes allowed as long as offensive players have touched the baseline.
3. Player who shoots the ball in the three-on-two phase or turns it over will sprint back downcourt on defense as the two defenders now attack him, two-on-one, passing the ball until they shoot a basic layup.

Upon completion of Phase 3, next set of five players will go back and repeat all phases. Correction of mistakes is an important aspect of practice in order to avoid poor transition game habits. All phases should be executed at game speed.

Full-Court Two-Minute Drill

Number of players needed: 9–10 players with one basketball

Drill time needed: Two minutes

Scoring: 16–18 average; 19–21 good; 22–23 very good; 24 perfect

Drill alignment: Players evenly divided in three lines, ball in middle (Figure 8.17)

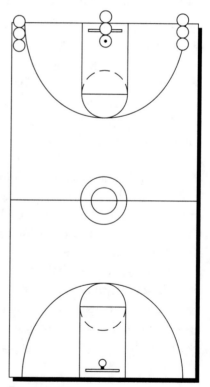

Figure 8.17

Basic Concepts Taught

★ Conditioning
★ Ballhandling
★ Execution

1. Ball is thrown to center jump circle using *baseball pass* to sprinting player from left line (Figure 8.18).
2. Passer sprints to other end to grab rebound. Right line is sprinting to opposite basket.
3. Player at center jump circle catches ball, pivots without traveling, and passes to sprinting shooter with a *chest pass* for a right-handed layup (Figure 8.19).
4. Shooter then sprints back to original basket.

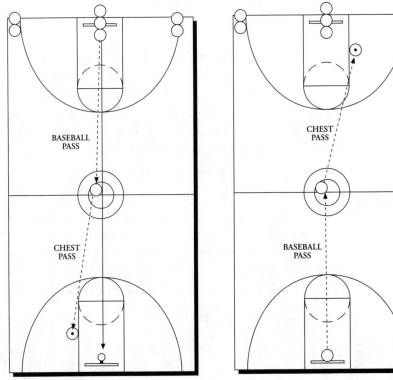

Figure 8.18   Figure 8.19

Seminole High School and Five-Star coaching legend Bob Traina in 2001

5. Rebounder gets ball out of basket and makes baseball pass again to center jump circle who catches ball, pivots without traveling, and passes to sprinting shooter with a chest pass for a right-handed layup at the original basket.
6. Lines rotate to the right.

The ball never touches the floor and dribbling or traveling are not allowed. Only layups count. A 12-man team can rotate completely through the drill in exactly two minutes, hence the drill's name and time selection.

Variation: switch shooting and passing lines so that all shots are left-handed layups.

Five-Star Off-Season Programs

Bob Hurley

St. Anthony's High School
Jersey City, New Jersey

The Off-Season Program for the Developing Player

All drills must be done at a high level of intensity.

Ten Modes of Individual Development

1. Jump rope/push-ups
2. Shooting warm-up
3. Quickness and agility drills
4. Shooting drills
5. Defensive drills
6. Ballhandling drills
7. Ballhandling moves with shooting
8. Rebounding drills
9. Perimeter and post moves
10. One-on-none or one-on-one

After every individual mode, shoot a total of five free throws.

1. *Jump Rope Drill:* jump rope 10 to 20 minutes a day.
   ★ Both feet
   ★ Right foot
   ★ Left foot
   ★ Alternating of feet
   ★ Boxer jumping
   ★ Five fingertip push-ups and 20 to 25 regular push-ups
2. *Quick Warm-Up Shooting Drill*
   ★ One arm
   ★ In close
   ★ Block-middle-block
3. *Quickness and Agility Drills:* from 30 seconds to one minute
   ★ Foul lane run
   ★ Box jump—four corners

    ★ Jump the line.

    ★ Skip the line.

    ★ Front and back jump

4. *Shooting Drills* (jump shot)

    ★ Roll the ball to the block; run and pick it up; pivot, square, and shoot.

    ★ Flip the ball to the block; run and pick it up; pivot, square, and shoot.

    ★ Roll the ball to the foul line; elbow run and pick it up; pivot, square, and shoot or drive.

    ★ Flip the ball out to the wing; run and pick it up; pivot, square, and shoot.

5. *Defense Drills*

    ★ Defense slides in the lane

    ★ Zig-zag slides

    ★ Run and cut off—run in zig-zag

    ★ Transition layup drill—shoot layup, rebound and put ball on ground, and then run to half-court, seeing the ball.

6. *Ballhandling Drills*

    ★ Dribble around right foot with right hand stationary.

    ★ Figure 8 through legs both stationary and moving

    ★ Dribble around left foot with left hand stationary.

    ★ Two-ball dribble in place, then with movement

    ★ Two-ball alternation dribbling

    ★ Two-ball dribble with one high and the other low

    ★ Rotation dribble

7. *Ballhandling Moves:* use both hands

    ★ Speed dribble—full court to basket in six dribbles or less; half-court to basket in three dribbles or less

    ★ Crossover

    ★ Between legs

    ★ Behind back

- ★ Inside out—hand exchange
- ★ Stutter step—stop/go move
- ★ 180 degree move, half-spin
- ★ Combination of all moves ending in a jump shot or drive. Shake and bake time!
- ★ Control dribble, same moves at slower paces.
- ★ Don't practice spin move often; it is only an open court move.

8. *Rebounding Drills*
   - ★ Albert King—rim touching: left, right, both hands, alternations of hands. Jump and see how many times you can touch the rim on the way up and on the way down. Then jump and touch the rim as many times as you can.
   - ★ Adrian Dantley—keep ball over head, pound on backboard five to 10 times, then take a power layup. Repeat drill five times. Next pound and move across the backboard and take a layup, then come back in the original direction.
   - ★ Moses Malone—throw ball on backboard, go up, and take power layup.
   - ★ Superman drill—start outside the paint, throw ball up on backboard, and jump for the rebound, keeping the ball over head and ending in a one-quarter turn at the other side of the paint. Turn and fake outlet pass, then repeat drill again.
   - ★ Tapping drill—jump up, tapping ball on backboard. First use both hands, then one hand.
   - ★ One-ball Mikan—hook shot in lane, alternating hands

9. *Perimeter and Post Moves*
   - ★ Perimeter moves—flip or roll ball out
   - ★ Jab-step series—jab-go, jab-jump, jab-scoop. Then cross into jump shots or drives such as reverse layups, inside hand

layups, and strong-side drive. Seal into baby block jump shot, power layup, and/or hook shot.

★ Post moves—flip or roll ball to block; middle post and high post

★ Six keys to posting up
   ★ Always post above block.
   ★ Stay low.
   ★ Don't rush.
   ★ Catch the ball—eye and hand contact
   ★ Chest and chin ball
   ★ Locate; square; toe up for pivot. Don't dribble.
      -Sikma—high in post, keep ball high over head; low in post, scoop cross the ball
      -Drop step—baseline or middle
      -Jump hook—sky hook

10. *One-on-None or One-on-One*
   ★ Play one-on-one perimeter with three to two dribbles or only one dribble.
   ★ Play one-on-one full-court with only eight to 10 dribbles.
   ★ Play one-on-one post up with only one dribble.
   ★ Play one-on-none. Use your mind and challenge yourself. Every made shot is plus one point, every missed shot is minus one point. Play to 10, 20, or 30. Example: plus 10 you win; minus 10 you lose. If you lose, discipline yourself: do push-ups, run laps or sprints, and so forth.

Shooting Techniques

★ Solo shooting—straight up in the air about 10 feet high
★ Coach Hurley's shooting drill
★ Develops shooting quickness because you get used to not dipping when you catch the ball

★ Start around the foul line—aim for a spot on the backboard. Shoot the ball.

★ Step back while ball is in the air—when bouncing to you, "load your hands," step, and shoot.

★ Keep hands up and step in when you can.

★ Coach Hurley's shooting drill with shot fake—same as previous, but shot fake first after catch.

Moves Facing the Basket

To develop various moves to attack the rim. (All moves are done from both the right and left elbow.)

Drill

★ Outside hand dribble, wrap ball behind back, layup

★ Outside hand dribble, two-foot jump-stop, power layup

★ Outside hand dribble, inside-out move, layup

★ Outside hand dribble, inside-out move, front change, layup on reverse side

★ Outside hand dribble, inside-out move, front change, jump shot

★ Outside hand dribble, inside-out, front change, baby hook over front rim

The key to your development is working out five to seven times a week during the off season and two to three times a week during the season. Your work must be hard, strenuous, and intense. Success only comes to those who work for it.

Be it cone, chair, or person, Bob Hurley Sr.'s intensity remains high-octane as he takes Honesdale campers through his summer program for the developing player. The future Springfield Hall of Famer, who put tiny St. Anthony's of Jersey City on the big-time basketball map, has won an astounding 90 percent of his games against top-notch competition over a 30-year period. The amazing number of guards he has developed includes his own sons Bobby and Danny. He was inducted into the Five-Star Hall of Fame in August 2002.

Tobin Anderson

Clarkson University
Clarkson, New York

Complete Workout for the Better Player

Guards

Ballhandling; make five free throws
Two-ball dribbling; make five free throws
Chill Drill (two times each hand); make five free throws
Guard moves; make five free throws
Point moves; make five free throws
Jumpers (make 25—have a partner pass to you or pass to yourself); make five free throws
Jumpers off dribble (make 25—have a partner pass to you or pass to yourself); make five free throws
Drives to basket (make 20—spin ball to self; vary your finishes); make five free throws
Post moves (make 20—spin ball to self; jump hooks, up-and-unders); make five free throws

★ Workout should take no more than 35 to 40 minutes
★ If you are with a partner, substitute partner shooting for spinning to self
★ Go at game speed, push yourself, make it tough
★ Run sprints for missed free throws (down and back)
★ *Shoot, shoot, shoot* on shoot-away

Stationary Ballhandling

★ Fingertip touches
★ Ball slaps (30)
★ Body circles (ankles, knees, waist, and head)

★ Up and down (head, waist, knees, and ankles)
★ Around two legs, around one
★ One hand in front, one hand behind
★ Two hands in front, two behind
★ Figure 8's
★ Full-body circles

Stationary Dribbling

★ Right-hand pound (high, low, front, back, and side)
★ Left-hand pound (high, low, front, back, and side)
★ Front to back, side to side (right and then left)
★ Crossovers
★ Behind-the-back crossovers
★ Killer crossovers (pound and cross)
★ Behind-the-back killer crossovers
★ Figure 8's
★ Spider

Two-Ball Dribbling and Game-Speed Drills

★ Juggle two balls
★ Juggle two off floor (B. J. Armstrong)
★ Pound two (high, low, front, back, side)
★ One ball high, one ball low
★ Out of rhythm (one, then the other)
★ Change hands

Post Players

Ballhandling and Mikan (forward and reverse) with heavy ball; make five free throws

Guard moves/point moves/change of speed (pick one); make five free throws

Tips, rips, rips with shot fake, slams (with heavy ball); make five free throws

Low-post moves (back to basket, drop
steps; hooks; up-and-unders; Barkley—
make 20); make five free throws

Low-post moves II (make 20—all Sikmas);
make five free throws

High-post moves (jumpers, onside,
crossovers); make five free throws

Perimeter jumpers (make 25—spin ball to
yourself) or partner shooting; make
five free throws

Jumpers off dribble (make 25—spin ball to
yourself) or partner shooting; make
five free throws

Drives to basket (make 20—spin to
yourself; vary your finishes); make five
free throws

★ Workout should take no more than 35 to
40 minutes
★ If you are with a partner, substitute
partner shooting for spinning to self
★ Go at game speed, push yourself, make it
tough
★ Run sprints for missed free throws (down
and back)
★ *Shoot, shoot, shoot* on shoot-away
★ Figure 8's
★ Random two-ball dribbling

Full-Court Dribbling (start at one end, go to
other, right hand down, left hand back)

★ Stop and go
★ Pull back and go (pull back two and then
go by in same hand)
★ Pull back crossover (go hard three, pull
back two and cross over and go)

Guard Moves

★ Between the legs
★ Behind the back

★ Crossover
★ Pull-back crossover

Point Moves

★ Inside out (half crossover)
★ Stutter step
★ Stop and go
★ Crossover
★ Behind back
★ Pull-up jumper (get the man in a chance,
  then shoot pull-up)

Ballhandling whiz Tobin Anderson (head coach at Clarkson University) pulls a dribbling trifecta as part of his summer program for the better player at RMC in Pittsburgh in July 2001.

How do you get to Carnegie Hall? Practice, practice, practice! Tobin Anderson proves this point with his "Impossible Catches" in July 2000.

Index

About the Authors

Howard Garfinkel and Will Klein cofounded the Five-Star Basketball Camp in 1966. More than 250 of their videotapes are on the market covering all aspects of the game, including coaching. More than two hundred campers have gone on to play at least one game in the NBA and 242 (and counting) high school coaches, camp workers, and college players have advanced to the college, junior college, or professional coaching ranks. The list of alumni campers and coaches is a *Who's Who* of the basketball world.

Mr. Garfinkel is on the McDonald's and Naismith Selection Committees and is cofounder and vice president of the New York City Basketball Hall of Fame and the "City Game." He was named Youth Mentor of the Millennium at the Horse Will Drink 2000 annual dinner in Pittsburgh. Mr. Klein is a retired New York City principal and former basketball coach at Christopher Columbus High School. Both men were inducted into the New York City Pro-Am Hall of Fame in 2001 and the Brooklyn Basketball Old-Timers of America Hall of Fame in 2002. In March 2003, they were inducted into the New York State Basketball Hall of Fame. In addition, the Five-Star Basketball Camp was presented with the Special Recognition Award for the camp's "significant work with the youth of America" by General Barry R. McCaffrey in Washington, D.C., on October 30, 1998.